Indian Roots
of
Judeo-Christianity
(Louis Jacolliot's Thesis Re-edited and Revised)

by
Dr. Ravi Prakash Arya

INDIAN FOUNDATION FOR VEDIC SCIENCE
H.O.1051, Sector-1, Rohtak, Haryana, India Ph. 01262-292580;
Delhi contact: 09313033917; 09650183260
vedicscience@hotmail.com
vedicscience@rediffmail.com
www.vedascience.com

First Edition

Kali era : 5115 (c. 2014)
Kalpa era : 1,97,29,49,115
Brahma era : 15,50,21,97,9,49,115

ISBN No. 81-87710-73-X

"As the most obscure solider of an army may sometimes by a fiery arrow destroy the strongest fortress of the enemy, so may the weakest man when he makes himself the courageous champion of truth, overthrow the most solid ramparts of superstition and of errors."

Manu, the first lawgiver of humankind

Contents

Editorial Note

Louis Jacolliot (1837-1890) worked in French India as a government official and was at one time President (Chief Judge) of the Court in Chandranagar. Jacolliot lived in India and studied Indian culture closely. He travelled extensively in India. Before his acquaintance with the Vedic literature in India, He also held the view, like other Europeans, that Europe is the cradle of world civilisations and the starting point of world history. According to him also, law of Justinian of Rome was the first written law of humankind. But his studies of Indian (Vedic) literature disapproved his assumptions and the truth was revealed to him that it was not Europe but India that had been the cradle of world civilisations. It was not the law of Justinian, but the Law of Manu that was the first written law of humankind. He was himself a Judge, so he could penetrate sharply into the truth and declare his academic Judgement which is unrivalled in the history of humankind.

Louis Jacolliot will be remembered in the line of those impartial researchers who accepted and announced truth for the sake of revealing truth and truth alone without any racial, regional or religious bias.

He had many books to his credit published in French, e.g.

1. *Les File De Dieu*

2. *Christna Et le Christ*

3. *Historie Des Verges*

4. *La Genese De L'humanite*

5. *Fetichisme - Polytheisme - Monotheisme*

6. *Le Spiritisme dans Le Monde*

7. *Les Traditions Indo- Asiatiques*

8. *Les Traditions Indo_ Europeennes*

9. *Le Pariah Dans L'humanite*

The present book is based upon the English Translation of Loius Jacolliot's original masterpiece in French titled as "*La Bible Dans L'Inde*". The book was published in 1876 in Paris by Librairie Internaionale, A Lacroix Et Cie Editeurs. Later its English translation was also published by G.W. Dillingham Publishers New York titled as "*Bible in India : Hindu Origin of Hebrews and Christian Revelations.*"

The Original book was divided in the four parts. Part first tries to project India as the cradle of World Civilisation. In this part, the author observes that India's contribution to the west was underestimated due to prejudiced views of the European scholars. Second part deals with the Indian Origin of Hebrew Society. Third part talks about the genesis of modern day religion of India. Fourth part deals with the Indian origin of Christianity.

The present book is a re-edited and revised edition in the sense that firstly it has not included the first part in it. It has already been reviewed in detail by the present editor in his earlier book "*India : The Cradle of the World Civilisations*". Moreover the first part being a general description of India's contribution to the western philosophy, ethics, language and laws, was not much relevant to the main theme of the present book "*Indian Roots of Judeo-Christinity*". So the present editor did not think it necessary to include the same in the present edition. Secondly, in the present edition, the sequence of parts has been changed in view of the subject matter dealt with herein. The second and third parts of the original book have been replaced with each other. This was done because the third part in original dealt with Genesis of the Indian religion that influenced the origin of western religions and second and fourth (in original book) dealt with the Indian elements in Judaism and Christianity. As such the genesis of Indian religion has been placed first in the present edition and bio-products have been discussed subsequently.

The most peculiar and salient feature of this edition is that the names of persons and places spelled by Jacolliot had French type of phonemic representation, as such Indian names with French type phonemic representation became difficult for purpose of pronunciation and comprehension by the readers. To overcome this problem, they have been spelt in a more modern way.

Moreover, sometimes Louis Jacolliot is not able to understand the Indian philosophy, culture and history in its true sense. So, all such places where untrue depiction of Indian philosophy, culture and history has occurred have been amended and updated. For example, he writes that Krishna was born to the virgin Devakī. This is a misconception. He also spells Devakī as Devanguy. So, here the whole story along with spellings have been amended. Similarly, all such discussions which do not support the main theme of the book and unnecessarily adding up to the pages of the book have been dropped.

Hope the readers will find this updated and revised version very interesting and more informative.

Dated: 7.11.2014   **Dr. Ravi Prakash Arya**

114-Akash, DRDO Complex,
Lucknow Road, Timarpur,
Delhi-110054 (India)
Ph. +91 9313033917; +91 9650183260
vedicscience@rediffmail.com
vedicscience@hotmail.com
www.vedascience.com

Preface
Louis Jacolliot

To religious despotism, imposing speculative delusions, and class-legislation, may be attributed the decay of nations. Spain is in the midst of her revolution against wax candles and holy water-let us suspend our judgement. Italy has not yet perfected the consolidation of her unity.

Rome is preparing in a General Council to denounce all conquests of modern intelligence freedom of thought, liberty of conscience, civil independence, etc.

Excommunication attempts to revivify its impotent thunders, and once more to bind emperors, kings, and people to its yoke.

English bishops strive in the name of Luther to establish a unity of dogma that shall make them powerful - and they proscribe Colenso.

England stifles the groans of Ireland.

The followers of Omar oppose and proscribe in Allah's name, the reforms that might save Turkey.

Poland exists no more, the Muscovite sword has realised the prediction of dying Kasciusco.

The Czar of Russia is Pope.

And yet - enter temple, church, or mosque, every where is intolerant persecution placed under the Aegis, of God.

It is no longer mediaeval fanaticism, for faith is dead; it is hypocrisy that thus rummages the arsenals of the past for arms, that may still have power to terrify the people once more to grovel on bended knees in the dust of credulity and darkness.

Yes! but liberty is a young and vigorous tree, and the more it is pruned the more vigorous will be its growth.

France alone possesses the principle of equality - its vital sap is always potent ; let her then advance without revolution and without violence, to the peaceful conquest of free institutions.

The unfailing result of force is to create divisions, and dread even of liberty's self; and thus to arrest progress.

But, wherefore, 'midst all the rumours that surround her from east to west, from north to south, does the sometimes seem to hesitate? Who impedes her march? What does she fear?

Is not the young generation, is not *New France* ready to abjure the impotence of a past which she will not restore, and boldly to follow the onward flag that shall ensure freedom within, and respect from without?

Then, forward!

The age of pulpits and religious agitators is past; we know the value of clerical oligarchies attached to power, and with what facility the principles of to-day's success are repudiated as antagonistic to-morrow.

We will no more place them in the curule chair.

And as we are en route, let us loyally and courageously assist the advance.

'Midst reviving intolerance, and all the religious strifes that divide Europe, I come to lay before you the life of a people whose laws, literature, and morale still pervade our civilisation, and whose grave was dug by sacerdotal hands.

I come to show you how humanity, after attaining the loftiest regions of speculative philosophy, of untrammelled reason on the venerable soil of India, was trammelled and stifled by the alter that substituted for intellectual life a semi-brutal existence of dreaming impotence.

The Council is about to assemble; all enemies of liberty are preparing for the great contest, and I rise to show whence their origin, whence derived their holy revelation, and to say to the Government of France-

Beware of the sacerdotal heritors of Hindu Brahmanism!

They, too, began with poverty and abnegation, and ended with opulence and despotism.

Listen to the Catholic Missionary *Dubois* on the ancient Brahmins. We cannot suspect him of partiality:

Justice, humanity, good faith, compassion, disinterestedness; in fact, all the virtues were familiar to them, and taught by them to other, both by precept and example : hence the Hindus profess, speculatively at least, nearly the same principles of morality as ourselves.*

Thus did they gain over the peoples, by making the divine precepts of Krishna a stepping-stone to power; and when the princes, who had assisted their success, sought to shake off their control, they but rose to succumb as slaves. Fearful lesson of the past, by which let the future profit!

India is the world's cradle; thence it is, that the common mother in sending forth her children even to the utmost West, has in unfading testimony of our origin bequeathed us the legacy of her language, her laws, her morale, her literature, and her religion.

Traversing Persia, Arabia, Egypt, and even forcing their way to the cold and cloudy North, far from the sunny soil of their birth; in vain they may forget their point of departure, their skin may remain brown, or become white from contact with snows of the West; of the civilisations founded by them splendid kingdoms may fall, and leave no trace behind but some few ruins of sculptured columns; new peoples may rise from the ashes of the first; new cities flourish on the site of the old; but time and ruin united fail to obliterate the even legible stamp of origin.

Science now admits, as a truth needing no further demonstration, that all the idioms of antiquity were derived from the far East; and thanks to the labours of Indian philologists, our modern languages have hound their derivation and their roots in Sanskrit.

It was but yesterday that the lamented Burn///ouf drew the attention of his class to our much better comprehension of the Greek and Latin, since we have commenced the study of Sanskrit.

And do we not now assign the same origin to Slavonic and Germanic languages?

Manu inspired Egyptian, Hebrew, Greek, and Roman legislation, and his spirit still permeates the whole economy of our European laws.

Cousin has somewhere said, The history of Indian philosophy is the abridged history of the philosophy of the world."

But this is not all.

Indian emigrants, together with their laws, their usage, their customs, and their language, carried with them equally their religion - their pious memories of the Gods of that home which they were to see no more- of those domestic gods whom they had burnt before leaving forever.

So, in returning to the fountain-head, do we find in India all the poetic and religious traditions of the Gods of that home which they were to see no more- of those domestic gods whom they had burnt before leaving forever.

So in returning to the fountain-head, do we find in India all the poetic and religious traditions of ancient and modern peoples. The worship of Zoraster, the symbols of Egypt, the mysteries of Eleusis and the priestesses of Vesta, the Genesis and prophecies of the Bible, the morale of the Samian sage, and the sublime teachings of the philosopher of Bethlehem.

This book comes to familiarise all those truths which have hitherto but agitated the higher regions of thought, those truths which, doubtless, many have perceived without daring to proclaim them.

It is the history of religious revelation, transmitted to all peoples, disengaged, as far as possible, from the fables of ignorance and designing Sacerdotalism of all times.

Aware of the resentment I am provoking, I yet shrink not from the encounter. We are no longer burnt at the stake, as in the times of Michael Servetus, Savonarola, and of Philip II. of Spain; and free thought may be freely proclaimed in an atmosphere of freedom. And thus do I submit my book to the reader.

The Voices of India.

Soil of Ancient India, cradle of humanity, hail! Hail, venerable and efficient nurse whom centuries of brutal invasions have not yet buried under the dust of oblivion' hail, father land of faith, of love, of poetry and of science. May we hail a revival of thy past in our Western future!

I have dwelt midst the depths of your mysterious forests, seeking to comprehend the language of your lofty nature, and the evening airs that murmured midst the foliage of Banyans words: Zeus, Jehova, Brahmā.

I have inquired of Brahmins and priests under the porches of temples and ancient pagodas; and they have replied.

"To live is to think, to think is to study God, who is all, and is in all."

I have listened to the instruction of pundits and sages, and they have said:

"To live is to learn, to learn is to examine and to fathom I all their perceptible forms the innumerable manifestation of celestial power."

I have turned to philosophers and have said to them:

"What then are you doing here, stationary, for more than six thousand years, and what is this book that you are always fumbling on your knees?"

And they have smiled in murmuring these words:

"To live is to be useful, to live is to be just, and we learn to be useful and just in studying this book of the Vedas, which is the word of eternal wisdom, the principle of principles as revealed to our fathers."

I have heard the songs of poets ș and love, beauty, perfumes and flowers, they two have afforded their divine instruction.

I have seen fakirs smiling at grief on a bed of thorns and of burning coals. - Suffering spoke to them of God.

I have ascended to the sources of the Ganges, where thousands of Hindus kneel, at the sun's rising, on the banks of the sacred river - and the breeze has borne to me these words:

" The fields are green with rice, and the coca- tree bends under its fruit- let us return thank to Him who gave them."

And yet, this earnest faith, these breathing beliefs, despite the sublime instruction of Brahmins, of sages, of philosophers and of poets, I have seen your sons, poor old Hindu mother, enervated, enfeebled, demoralised by brutish passions, abandon, without complaint to a handful of grinding merchants, your blood, your wealth, your virgin daughters, and your liberty.

How often have not hear on the evening air, hoarse moans of wailing complaint that seemed to rise from desert marshes, sombre pathways, rivers' banks, or woody shades, & c. ! Was it the voice of the past, returning to weep o'er a lost civilisation and an extinguished grandeur?

Was it the expiring groan of Sepoys mowed down pell-mell by grape with their wives and children after the revolt, by some red-jackets who thus revenged their own panic?

Was it the wail of nurselings, vainly seeking sustenance at the cold breast of mothers - dead from starvation?

Alas! what fearful sufferings has it been my fate to

witness!

A people smiling in apathy under the iron hand that destroys them, and with their own hand joyously digging the grave of their ancient glories, of their recollections and of their independence.

What sinister influence, I asked myself, has then been the cause of such a state of decomposition? Is it simply the work of time, and is it the destiny of nations, as of man, to die of decrepitude?

How is it that the primeval doctrines, the sublime instruction of the Vedas have ended in such a failure?

And still I heard Brahmins and sages, philosophers and poets, "in solemn converse" on the immortality of the soul, on the great social virtues, and on the Divinity!

And still I saw the populations bend before Him who gave their cloudless sun and fertile soil!

At least, however, I perceived that it was, alas! but an empty from. .. And I saw with sadness that these people had bartered the spirit of their sublime beliefs for a verbal fanaticism, freedom of thought and the free will of free men for the blind and stolid submission of the slave.

Then it was that I sought to lift the obscuring veil from the past, and backwards trace the origin of this dying people, who without energy for either hatred or affection, without enthusiasm for either virtue or vice, seem to personate an actor doomed to act out his part before an audience of Statues.

How glorious the epoch that then presented itself to my study and comprehension! I made tradition speak from the temple's recess, I inquired of monuments and ruins, I questioned the Vedas whose pages count their existence by thousands of years, and whence inquiring youth imbibed the science of life long before Thebes of the hundred gates or Babylon the great had traced out their foundations.

I listened to recitals of those ancient poems which were

sung at the feet of Brahma when the shepherds of Upper Egypt and of Judea had not yet been born. . . . I sought to understand those laws of Manu which were administered by Brahmins under the porches of pagodas ages and ages before the tables of the Hebrew law had descended midst thunders and lightning from the heights of Sinai.

And then did India appear to me in all the living power of her originality - I traced her progress in the expansion of her enlightenment over the world - I saw her giving her laws, her customs, her morale and her religion to Egypt, to Persia, to Greece and to Rome - I saw Jaiminī and Vedavyāsa precede Socrates and Plato, - and Christna (Krishna), the son of Devakī, precede the son of the Virgin of Bethlehem.

This was the epoch of greatness, under the regime of reason.

And then I followed the footsteps of decay . . . old age approached there people who had instructed the world, and impressed upon it their morale and their doctrines with a seal so ineffaceable, that time, which has entombed Babylon and Nineveh, Athens and Rome, has not yet been able to obliterate it.

I saw Brahmins and priests lend the sacerdotal support of voice and sacred function to the stolid despotism of kings-- and ignoring their own origin, stifle India under a corrupt the ocracy that soon extinguished the liberty that would have been its overthrow, as the memory of those past glories which were its reproach.

And then I saw clearly why there people, after two thousand years of religious thraldom, were powerless to repulse their destroyers and demand retribution, bowing passively to the hated domination of English merchants ş while night and morning on bended knees imploring that God in whose name Sacerdotalism had effected their ruin.

Chandranagar, West Bengal

PART FIRST

GENESIS OF INDIAN RELIGIOUS CONCEPTS THAT INFLUENCED THE ORIGIN OF WESTERN RELIGIONS

I
ZEUS AND BRAHMĀ — RELIGIOUS COMICAL BELIEFS

Early writers who occupied themselves with the Indians and their religious dogmas, ill-instructed, ignorant of the language of the country, and influenced by pre-adopted ideas, devoted themselves only to the exposure of a worship, apart, to a certain extent, from the religious idea, vary according to the imagination and character of the people.

They did not perceive that they were in a worn out country whose *decadence* already dated back some three or four thousand years; that the pure beliefs of primitive ages had been replaced by innumerable poetic legends and myths, and that it was necessary to penetrate the interior of temples, to inquire of tradition, to consult learned Brahmins, and force from records their secrets, to arrive at a comprehension of the splendour of the past and the degradation of the present.

After them come those indefatigable inquirers — the honour of our age, such as Strange, Colebrooke, Weber, Schlegel, Burnouf, Desgranges, and others, who exhumed to the eyes of an astonished world, the primitive language from which ancient and modern idioms are descended.

We began to perceive the truth with regard to this ancient country which was the cradle of the white race; but until then we had but occupied ourselves in translating fragments of the numerous philosophic works and grand poems which India had bequeathed us, rather than in identifying the primitive idea that had given birth to philosophic science and to the religious myths of poetry.

The pure Indian religion recognises and admits but one only God, thus defined by the Veda— "Him who exists by himself, and who is in all, because all is in him."

Manu, annotating the Veda, says: "Him who exists by himself, whom the spirit alone can perceive, who is imperceptible to the organs of sense, who is without visible parts, eternal, the soul of all beings, and whom none can comprehend."

The *Mahābhārata* also gives the following definition:

"God is one, immutable, without form or parts, infinite, omnipresent, and omnipotent; He made the heavens and the worlds to spring forth from infinite void, and launched them into boundless space; He is the divine mover, the great originating essence, the efficient and material cause of all."

Let us again here the Veda, that in a poetic burst exclaims:

"The Ganges that flows — it is God; the ocean that roars — it is God; the wind that blows — it is Him ; the cloud that thunders, the lightning that flashes — it is Him. As from all eternity the universe existed in the spirit of Brahmā, so to-day is all that exists his image."

I do not think that the lapse of ages, and what we conventionally call the development of the human mind, has added anything to these definitions.

Indian theologians distinguish God in two different situations:

In the first he is Zeus (Devas), that is, God, not operating, not yet revealed.

It is of him that the *Purāṇas* have said, in their commentaries on the holy books:

"Spirit mysterious! force immense! power immeasurable! now was your power, your force, your life manifested before the period of creation?

"Didst thou sleep like an extinguished sun in the bosom of decomposing matter? Was that decomposition in thee, or didst thou ordain it? Wert thou chaos? Wert thou life, comprehending in thee all the lives that had fled the strife of destroying elements? If thou wast life, thou wast also destruction, for destruction comes from action, and action existed not without thee."

"Hadst thou cast the moldering worlds into a fiery furnace to purify and reproduce them from decomposition ; as the decaying tree is born again from its seed which develops its germs in the bosom of rottenness?

"Did thy spirit float upon the waters; since thou art called Nārāyaṇa?"

This name of Nārāyaṇa furnishes another instance of singular affinity of expression with the Bible — further proofs to be added to all the others of the Indian origin of the Bible.

Let us first explain the word, but let Manu speak (Book Ist)

"The waters have been named Naras because they were the production of Nara (in Sanskrit, the Divine Spirit), these waters having been the first scene of Nara's unquiescence (in Sanskrit, Ayana). He (Brahmā) was in consequence named Nārāyaṇa — him who moves upon the waters."

Bible, Genesis, chapter i.

"Terra autem erat inanis et vacua.

"Et spiritus Dei ferebatur super aquas."

" The earth was in formed and naked."

"And the spirit of God moved upon the waters."

Nara, the divine Spirit; *Ayana*, that moves himself (on the waters); Spiritus Dei, the divine Spirit; *ferebatur super aquas,* was borne upon the waters!

It is sufficiently clear, sufficiently evident? Could book or Bible be more distinctly caught in the act of imitation?

There remains but one mode of escape, it is to deny the Sanskrit: nothing is impossible, but we shall see.

In the second situation Zeus becomes Brahmā, that is God

revealed, and operating, God the Creator.

Again, let the *Purāṇas* speak:

"When Brahmā passed from inaction to action, he came, not to create nature, which existed from all time in its essence and its attributes in his immortal thought, he came to develop it and to arrest dissolution.

"O God, creating Father, in what form clothest thou thyself, in action? the works of thy grandeur, of thy powerful will, astonish our perception; the ocean raises its furious billows and subsides, the thunder resounds and is still, the wind moans and it passes, man is born and dies, everywhere do we feel thy hand which protects and commands, but we can neither comprehend it, nor see it."

Must we deny first cause? Who has ever dreamt of denying his thought, because he cannot see it?

I don't know if those gentlemen of Rome will find all this sufficiently orthodox; for me, I feel myself penetrated with an admiration beyond comparison, for those sacred books which give me an idea of God so *grandiose*, and so free from all those imperfections with which certain men have surcharged it in other climes, in attributing to him their own thoughts, and above all in making the Supreme Being the auxiliary of their ambitions.

According to Indian belief, matter is subject to the same laws of existence and decomposition as vegetables and animals; after a certain period of life, comes the period of dissolution, everything decays, all returns to chaos: the harmony of worlds is at an end — air, earth, water, light, commingle and become extinct: it is the *Pralaya*, or destruction of all that exists; but there is a germ which purifies itself by repose, until the day when Brahmā again comes to develop it, to give it life, the creative power, and to produce the worlds, which commence little by little, to form, to grow, and to operate, again to encounter a new decomposition, followed by the same repose and by the same regeneration.

Intrinsic law of matter, which fades by existence, grows old and dies — but is restored and vivified by God.

Astonishing fact! The Indian revelation, which proclaims the slow and gradual formation of worlds, is of all revelations the only one whose ideas are in complete harmony with modern science!

If Moses in his intercourse with the priests of Egypt knew of these sublime traditions, we must suppose that he considered them too lofty, too much above the intelligence of the slave people whom he had to direct, to be communicated to them. Perhaps, also, as we have already conjectured, he may himself have been only partially initiated in Egypt.

The period of action and re-construction of the worlds occupies, according to the Veda, one entire day of Brahmā — and that day corresponds to four millions three hundred and twenty thousand human years.

The *Pralaya,* or epoch of dissolution, lasts one entire night of Brahmā, and that night is equal to the same number of human years as the divine day.

These doctrines of holy books on the destruction and re-construction of worlds, have given birth to a crowd of philosophic systems which we have neither the time nor the desire here to study. We shall be content to indicate the two theories which, in all times, divided the theological schools of India on this subject.

The first maintains that the germs of matter, once fecundated by Brahmā, the phenomena of transformation operate spontaneously, and without direct participation of God, in accordance with the eternal and immutable laws which he has created.

Matter, in precipitating itself from its centre, from its generating focus, subdivides and gravitates in space; all particles are vapours which exhale produce atmospheric air and water. The fragments become habitable worlds.

Gradually all the other particles, according to their magnitude, become extinguished in their turn; but in proportion on as they become habitable, heat and light diminish, until having wholly disapperared–Matter, deprived of its most active agents of life and reproduction, falls back into chaos, into the night of Brahmā.

This opinion, which is not contradicted by the Veda, is nevertheless attacked by the orthodox, who accord to divine influence a more active role.

They recognise perfectly that it is thus nature develops herself, the elements form themselves; all the phenomena of existence accomplish themselves; that the worlds and matter thus likewise end, and lose themselves in the night of Brahmā.

But, according to them, God is the supreme law of all these phenomena, and exists in that law. He presides constantly at all these transformations, which would promptly cease to pursue their course, should he happen, even for an instant, to suspend his direction, to withdraw his support.

Indian priests cannot receive ordination without first declaring themselves partisans of this latter system, which is considered to be, much more than the first, in the religious spirit.

The book of Moses, occupied, solely with coarse fact, pays no attention to these theories, which form the basis of Oriental theology. Modern religions have placed them among their mysteries.

II

THE AWAKENING OF BRHAMĀ– CREATION OF DEVAS— THEIR REVOLT — THE VANQUISHED WERE CAST INTO HELL UNDER THE NAME OF RAKṢASAS OR DĀNAVAS

We have declared that it was from India emanated, by emigrations, all the religious myths at the base of all religions, ancient and modern; and certainly not without interest will be read this legend of the Vedas, which has been adopted unaltered by Christianity, without indicating the source whence it was drawn.

As the night of Brahmā approached its end before proceeding to create this world, and to cover it with plants and animals, the Lord of all things having divided the heavens into twelve parts, resolved to people them with beings proceeding from Himself, and to whom he might confide some of His attributes and a portion of his power.

"And having said: I will that the heavens people themselves with inferior spirits who shall obey me, and testify to my glory, the angels sprung forth from His thought, and hastened to arrange themselves around His throne."

As these spirits were created in a hierarchic order of power and perfection, God followed the same rule in assigning to each his dwelling; He placed the most perfect among the Devas in the interstellar space nearest Himself, and the others (planets) in the more distant space.

But scarcely had He given His order when a violent quarrel arose in Interstellar space the who had been assigned habitations in the most distant heavens, refused to go, and having placed Vāsukī (Planets are called Vāsukī as they are habitat of the living beings-editor) at their head, who had first excited them to revolt, they fell upon the better endowed

Devas (attracted by stars) to seize the heritage assigned them. The above story of fight between devas (stars) and danvas (planets) in the dyuloka (interstellar Space) tells about the phenomenon of origin of stars and planets from the solar nebula. The fight indicates the phenomenon of attraction and distraction between stars and planets. Planets could not exist independently. They were attracted by stars with comparatively story gravitation force. Stars were called Devas, as they had not light of their own. Planets are called Danvas, as they had not light of their own. They were rather called as Vāsukī, as they sustained biological life upon them.

These last, having ranged themselves under the banner of Indra, bravely sustained the shock, and the battle was waged in the presence of Brahmā, who did nothing to stop it.

Vāsukī having been overthrown by Indra, all his companions, terrified, abandoned him, declaring themselves ready to submit to the will of Brahmā; but he, irritated by their disobedience, chased them from interstellar space and interdicting equally earth and the other planets, left them only hell for a dwelling place. And he named them Rākṣasas, that is to say, the cursed.

Hence are born all those Dānvas (Planets), who, under the name of Rākṣasas, Nagas, Sarpas, Piśachs, an Asuras, officiate in Indian poetry, which represents them as unceasingly disturbing the *Yajñas* and devotions of mortals, who are obliged to call in the devas or angels, as well as holy personages, to their succour.

Hence also the myth of the archangel Michael! It did not astonish me to find this legend in India.

I had long considered unworthy of the Supreme Being this creation of a sort of demi-gods, who, scarce, emerged from naught, rise in opposition to the divine authority, and under its eyes, engage in a contest instigated by pride and the ambition to equal his power.

Before understanding India and its received myths, from

which have sprung all the others, I already knew that all ancient mythologies had admitted this revolt of the first created beings against the Creator, and that it was thus they accounted for the descent of the spirit of evil upon earth.

The struggle of the Titans against Jupiter, in the Greek Olympus, had certainly no other significance than to explain the birth of good and evil, and the influence of these two principles on nature.

Only, Greek mythology, derived from India, through Asia,— unconscious of primitive beliefs and the Vedas, was but an emanation of poetic legends, which infinitely subdivided the ancient proem; whereas Christianity recovered in Egypt the primitive tradition, free from the exaggerations invented by Oriental imagination.

But, ignoring India, we may still say that Hebrew and Christian revelations *revealed nothing*; what does it signify, in fact, whether you call the revolters against God, Titans or Angles? It can only provoke a contest about words; the principle and the idea are the same.

Primitive men, witnessing the existence of evil amongst them, too often, unhappily, triumphant over the good, would have sought also to explain it; and unable to assign it to God, who idealised the good, they could only find its origin in a struggle of the first creature produced by his goodness, against God himself.

Be this as it may, from India alone came the antique tradition which we find the same in the Noses of Zoroaster, and which seems but to have been imagined as an explanation of these two principles, of good and evil, which divide the world.

Untrammelled thought, in purifying and simplifying its belief, must reject this myth as inconsistent with the dignity of God, his presence, and his sovereign power.

The more we reject imagination and poetry, the more will our idea of the Creator become worthy of him.

Let us not seek the origin of evil elsewhere than in the weakness of human nature: there begins the mystery; it is there that we can no longer comprehend the motives of the Supreme Being. But instead of explaining them by absurd fables, or denying them by an opposite excess, let us abstain and confide in the inexhaustible goodness of Him who has not thought it expedient to initiate as in his designs.

If the light He has given us be weak, let reason fearlessly follow it! Demi-gods, revelateurs, and prophets, have given us nothing, taught us nothing, which that light had not given, and taught, before them. And, if we owe them anything, it is for the efforts made by themselves and their successors to *extinguish* the healthy doctrines of free will and conscience.

III

INDIAN TRINITY – ITS ROLE – CREATION OF THE EARTH

When the period of the "*Pralaya*" (dissolution) was complete, Brahmā, according to the expression of Manu, appeared resplendent in the éclat of this purity, and diffusing his own splendour, dissipated obscurity, and developed nature, having resolved, in his own thought, to produce all creatures from his substance.

Bhagavadagītā says:

"When the profound night, during which the germ of all things was regenerating itself in the bosom of Brahmā, dispersed, an immense light pervaded infinite space, and the celestial spirit appeared in all the strength and power of his Majesty: at sight of him chaos was changed into a fruitful womb, about to bring forth the worlds, the resplendent stars, the waters, the plants, animals, and men."

At the moment, when Zeus, unrevealed, unoperating became Brahmā, that is, the operating and creating God, three persons, reveal themselves in him to aid in his work, without, however, affecting his unity.

This divine Trimurti (Trinity), say the Brahmins and the sacred books, is indivisible in essence, and indivisible in action — mystery profound! which man will only comprehend when his soul shall be admitted to unite itself to the universal soul in the bosom of the divinity.

The Trinity consists of Brahmā, Viṣṇu, and Śiva.

Brahmā represents the creative principle, and receives, in Sanskrit the name of Father.

Viṣṇu represents the protecting and preserving principle,

he is the Son of God, the incarnate word in the person of Christna (Krishna), who comes upon earth, both pastor and prophet, to save humanity, then to die, his work accomplished, of a violent, ignominious death.

Lastly, Śiva or Nara, that is to say, the Divine Spirit — is the principle that presides at destruction and re-constitution, image of Nature, uniting the attributes of fecundity and of life of decomposition and of death. It is, in a word, the Spirit that directs that eternal movement of existence and of dissolution, which is the law of all beings.

The function of this Trinity commences from the first act of Creation — Brahmā creates, Viṣṇu protects or preserves, and Śiva transforms, and God continues to operate in his triple attributes until a new dissolution of nature until the day when all existence ends, and all returns to chaos.

According to Vedic revelation, matter is subject to one only law, which operates alike in all bodies, in all plants, and in all animals.

Thus a seed is thrown onto the earth, a germ is developed, it produces a plant, or a tree. This plant, or tree, grows, declines, dies, and returns to earth. But this plant, or this tree, has produced seed, which in its turn reproduces the original type which has disappeared. It is the same with animals, and with all that exists.

In the same way, matter, born of a germ fecundated by the Supreme Being, develops itself by fixed laws, and ends like the plant, the tree, and the animal, in decomposition. But a germ remains, which regenerates itself, fecundates itself anew in the bosom of the great soul of power supreme, and, anew, gives birth to the universe.

During this period the Trinity is lost in Unity as if non-existent, since unrevealed in action.

What charms me in this Indian belief is that it leads all back to unity, an accepts all the logical consequence. And how sublime in its simplicity is that great law of matter.

We may, I imagine, explore in vain, all religious, all philosophic systems, for ideas so rational, so much in conformity with the laws of nature and the dignity of God.

Let us now examine the work of this Trinity under the supreme direction of Brahmā.

From matter, God first produced ether air, light and water and earth.

Then from the Supreme soul, he emitted the life, or Mahān common to plants, animals and man, then the *ahaṁkāra*, that is conscience, the individual mind (le moi) with all its faculties, to be the special appendage of man alone.

Next, to distinguish the operation of conscience, he established the just, and the unjust, and gave thought to this individual mind (*à ce moi*), which was destined to guide the reasoning creatures he was about to produce from his substance.

After that God created plants, trees, and animals, and when according to the holy books, all nature was but one chorus of love, and of acknowledgement, Brahmā formed the man and the woman out of the purest of himself, and this done, he rested and admired himself in his work.

The abridged Manu, mutilated by the Brahmins to suit their newly established system, has not the simplicity and grandeur of the Veda: on these matters, however, we may say that following passages, although imperfect and unfaithful, are an echo of the primitive doctrine:

"When God awakes, then does the universe accomplish its operations; — when he sleeps — the spirit plunged in profound repose, then does the world dissolve.

"For during his tranquil sleep, animated beings, endowed with principles of action, forego their functions and sensation, that is, life, becomes inert."

"And when together dissolved in the supreme soul then does this soul of all beings sleep tranquilly in the most perfect repose."

"After retiring into primitive obscurity, if long retains the organs of sense, it accomplishes not its function, and divests itself of its form."

"When, reuniting anew the subtle elementary principles, it introduces itself into matter, then does it assume a new form."

"It is thus by alternate waking and repose that the Supreme Being eternally revives or dissolves all this assemblage of creatures, moving and motionless."

God is characterised by there attributes: as originator Brahmā, as sustainer Viṣṇu and as destroyer Śiva they have strayed from it.

According to Indian philosophical belief above many others, this logical side of conceiving that God manifests himself on earth whenever the weakness or the errors of humanity takes place, some great soul reincornate to guide the humanity or the path of *Dharma*.

The Trinity in Unity, rejected by Moses, became afterward the foundation of Christian theology, which incontestably acquired if from India.

Proofs sufficient will, in their proper place, establish this opinion.

IV

CREATION OF MAN

Wander throughout the South of India and the Island of Ceylon, where tradition is preserved in all its purity, inquire of the Indian in his humble straw hut, or of the priest in his temple; all will repeat to you this legend of the creation of man, as we are here about to relate it from the Veda. In the Bhagvada-Gitā Christna (Krishna) recalls it in a few words to his disciple and faithful co-adjutor Arjuna, and nearly in the same terms as in the sacred books.

The passages between inverted commas are simple translation from the text.

The earth was covered with flowers, the trees bent under their fruit, thousands of animals sported over the plains and in the air, white elephants roved unmolested under the shade of gigantic forests, and Brahmā perceived that the time had come for the creation of man, to inhabit this dwelling-place.

He drew from the great Soul, from the pure essence, a germ of life, with which he animated the two persons whom he made, male and female, that is proper for reproduction like plants and animals; and he gave them the *ahaṁkāra* (egotism) and speech, which rendered them superior to all he had yet created, but inferior to the Devas.

He distinguished the man by strength, shape, and majesty, and named him *Ādima* (in Sanskrit, the first man).

The woman received grace, gentleness, and beauty, and he named her Heva (in Sanskrit, what completes life).

Therefore, in giving *Ādima* a companion, the Lord perfected the life bestowed on him, and in thus establishing the conditions under which humanity was about to be born, he proclaimed on earth and in heaven the equality of the man and the woman.

Divine principle, which has been more or less misunderstood by legislations, ancient and modern, and which India only abandoned under the deleterious influence of priests at the Brahmanical revolution.

The Lord then gave to *Ādima* and to his wife Heva the primeval *Taprobane* of the ancients, The island of Ceylon (0° Longitude), for a residence, well-fitted, from its climate, its products, and its splendid vegetation, to be the terrestrial paradise, cradle of the human race.

It is still, to-day, the loveliest pearl of the Indian Seas.

"Go, said he, unite, and produce beings who shall be your living image upon earth, for ages and ages after you have returned to me. I, Lord of all that exists, have created you to worship me throughout your life, and those who shall have faith in me shall share my happiness after the end of all things. Thus instruct your children that they forget me not, for I shall be with them while they continue to call upon my name."

Then he forbid *Ādima* and Heva to quit Ceylon and continued in these terms:

"Your mission is confined to peopling this magnificent island, where I have gathered together everything for your pleasure and convenience; and to implant my worship in the hearts of those to be born.... The rest of the world is as yet uninhabitable; if hereafter the number of your children so increase as to render this habitation insufficient to contain them, let them inquire of me in the midst of *Yajña*, and I will make known my will."

Having said this, he disappeared.

"*Ādima* them turned towards his young wife ..... who stood before him, erect and smiling in her virgin candor.

"Clasping her in his arms, he gave her the first kiss of love if softly murmuring the name of Heva ... Ādima! softly whispered the woman, as she received the kiss....

"Night was come. The birds were silent in the trees. The Lord was satisfied, for the birth of love has preceded the union of the sexes.

"Thus had Brahmā willed it, to teach his creatures that the union of the man and the woman without love would be but an immorality, contrary to nature and to his law.

"*Ādima* and Heva lived for some time in perfect happiness – no suffering came to disturb their quietude; they had but to stretch forth the hand and pluck from surrounding trees the most delicious fruits, but to stoop and gather rice of the finest quality."

"But one day a vague disquietude began to creep upon them; — jealous of their felicity and of the work of Brahmā, the Prince of the Rākṣasas, the Spirit of Evil, inspired them with disturbing desires. 'Let us wander through the island,' said *Ādima* to his companion, 'and see if we may not find some place even more beautiful than this.'

"Heva followed her husband; they wandered for days and for months, resting beside clear fountains, under gigantic Banyan that protected them from the sun's rays... But as they advanced the woman was seized with strange fears, inexplicable terrors: *Ādima*, said to her, 'let us go no farther; it seems to me that we are disobeying the Lord. Have we not already quitted the place which he assigned us as a dwelling?"

"And they journeyed on.

"Arriving at last at the extremity of the Laṅkā, they beheld a smooth and narrow arm of the sea, and beyond it a vast and apparently boundless country, connected with Laṅkā by a narrow and rocky pathway arising from the bosom of the waters.

"The tow wandered stood amazed; the country before them was covered with stately trees, birds of a thousand colours fitting midst their foliage.

"Behold, what beautiful things!' cried *Ādima*, 'and what

good fruits such trees must produce! let us go and taste them, and if that country is better than this, we will dwell there.'

"Heva, trembling, besought *Ādima* to-do nothing that might irritate the Lord against them. 'Are we not well here? Have we not pure water and delicious fruits? Wherefore seek other things?'

" 'True,' replied *Ādima*, 'but we will come back; what harm can it be to have visited this unknown country, that presents itself to our view?'

"And approaching the rock, Heva, trembling, followed.

"Then, placing his wife upon his shoulders, he proceeded to cross the space that separated him from the object of his desires.

"But no sooner did they touch the shore, than trees, flowers, fruit, birds, all that they had seen from the opposite side, vanished in an instant midst terrific clamour; the rocks by which they had crossed sunk beneath the waters, a few sharp peaks alone remaining above the surface to indicate to place of the bridge, which had been destroyed by Divine displeasure."

Those rocks rise in the Indian Ocean between the eastern point of India and Laṅkā, are still known in that country under the name of *Palam Ādima*, i.e., Bridge of *Ādima*.

When steamers, bound for China and India, have passed the Maldives, the first point they discern of the Indian coast is a bluish peak, often crowned with clouds, which rises majestically from the bosom of the waters. The foot of this mountain was, according to tradition, the first man's point of departure for the continental coast.

From earliest times this mountain has borne the name of Adam's Peak, and under this name does modern geography still describe it.

Let us close this parenthesis, to continue our text.

"The vegetation which they had seen from far, was but a

delusive mirage, raised by the evil instincts to tempt them to disobedience.

"*Ādima* threw himself, weeping, upon the naked sands, but Heva came to him, and threw herself into his arms, saying, 'Do not despair; let us rather pray to the Author of all things, to pardon us.'

"And as she thus spoke there came a voice from the clouds, saying:

" 'Woman, thou hast only sinned from love to thy husband, whom I commanded thee to love, and thou hast hoped in Me I pardon thee, and him also for thy sake! But you may no more return to the abode of delight which I had created for your happiness. Through your disobedience to my commands, the spirit of evil has obtained possession of the earth. Your children, reduced to labour and to suffer by your fault, will become corrupt and forget Me. But I will send Viṣṇu, who shall incarnate himself in the womb of a woman, and shall bring to all the hope and the means of recompense in another life, in praying to Me to soften their ills.'

"They arose consoled, but ever after subjected by painful labour, to obtain their subsistence from the earth," (Ramatsariar, texts and commentaries on the Vedas.) How grand, how logical, and how simple, this beautiful Indian legend!

The Redeemer, Krishna, will be born of a woman to reward Heva, 'or having neither despaired of God, nor had the first idea of offence, in which she was only an accomplice from love to him whom the Creator had commanded her to love.

This is beautiful and consoling.

Behold here the veritable Eve, and we understand that one of her daughters may afterwards become the mother of a redeemer.

How is it that the awkward composer of the Hebrew

Genesis could not transcribe this version without mutilation?

Was it from forgetfulness or design, that the woman is charged by Moses with the whole weight of original sin?

We hesitate not to declare it intentional, and from cowardly deference to the manners of the age, that the Hebrew legislator thus falsified the ancient tradition of the East. In our next chapter will be found our justification of this conclusion.

But what are we to think of this legend?

However seductive it may appear, reason must alike reject it, in either Indian culture or Christian religion.

We cannot attribute such weakness to God, as to believe that for a simple an single transgression of our first parents, he could condemn entire unfolding humanity to suffering and sin.

This tradition was a needful invention:

The early races of men, feeling all the ills they had to support, perceiving their own weakness, their nature composed of good and evil instincts; instead of cursing God who had created them, preferred to seek in primitive transgression the justification of their miserable condition. Hence that original sin which we find in all the beliefs of all the peoples of our globe; even amongst the savage tribes of Africa and of Oceanica.

Perhaps, also, it may be but a souvenir of the easy and happy life of the ancient inhabitants of the globe, at a time when the earth, less charged with population, afforded in abundance, and without labour, all things necessary for subsistence.

V

THE WOMAN OF THE VEDAS AND THE WOMAN OF BIBLE

India of the Vedas entertained a respect for women, amounting to worship; a fact which we seem little to suspect in Europe when we accuse the extreme East of having denied the dignity of woman, and of having only made of her an instrument of pleasure and of passive obedience.

What was true of antiquity, was not so with regard to ancient India; and the sublime efforts of Christ did but restore to woman the social position which she had enjoyed in the earliest ages of humanity.

Let it be well understood, that it was but sacerdotal influence and Brahmanical decay that, in changing the primitive conditions of the East, reduced woman to a state of subordination which has not yet wholly disappeared from our social system.

Let us read these maxims taken at hazard from the sacred books of India.

"Man is strength — woman is beauty; he is the reason that governs, but she is the wisdom that moderates; the one cannot exist without the other, and hence the Lord created them two, for the one purpose.

"Man is incomplete without woman, and the man who does not marry at the age of virility should be stigmatised as infamous."

"He who despises woman, despises his mother."

"Who is cursed by woman, is cursed by God."

"The tears of a woman call down the fire of heaven on those who make them flow."

"Evil to him who laughs at woman's sufferings, God shall

laugh at his prayers."

"The songs of women are sweet in the ears of the Lord; men should not, if they wish to be heard, sing the praises of God without women."

"The priest shall allow women to burn perfume upon the altar, when he performs *yajña* for fruits, for flowers, for households, and for creation."

"Women should be protected with tenderness, and gratified with gifts, by all who wish for length of days."

"It was at the prayer of a woman that the Creator pardoned man; cursed be he who forgets it."

"A virtuous woman needs no purification, for she is never defiled, even by contact of impurity."

"Who shall forget the sufferings of his mother at his birth, shall be re-born in the body of an owl during three successive transmigrations."

"There is no crime more odious than to persecute women, and to take advantage of their weakness to despoil them of their patrimony.

"In assigning her portion to his sister, each brother should add to it, from his own; and present to her the finest heifer of his herd, the purest saffron of his crop, the most beautiful jewel of his casket."

"The woman watches over the house, and the protecting divinities (Devas) of the domestic hearth are happy in her presence. The labours of the field should never be assigned her."

"Woman should be for man the soother of labour and the consolation of misfortune."

The sentiments expressed in these citations are not isolated, or only found in one work; all Indian ancient books are filled with the same love, the same respect for woman. The abridgement of Manu, constructed by the Brahmins in support of their own ideas of domination, although placing woman in a position more subordinate, more obscure, could not, in many circumstances, escape making itself the echo of those primitive principles which might not be so soon forgotten.

We have, in fact, already cited a passage from this book, which we think it not inappropriate here to reproduce:

"Women should be shielded with fostering solicitude by their fathers, their brothers, their husbands, and the brothers of their husbands, if they hope for great prosperity."

"Wherever women live in affliction, the family becomes extinct, but where they are loved, respected, and surrounded with tenderness, the family increases, and prospers in every way."

"When women are honoured, the divinities are content, but where they are not honoured, all undertaking fail"

"The households cursed by women, to whom they have not rendered the homage due them, find themselves weighed down with ruin and destroyed, as if they had been struck by some secret power."

"In households where the husband is content with his wife and the wife with her husband, happiness is ensured forever."

We also read in the same work:

"When relatives, by some subterfuge, take possession of the property of a woman, her carriages, or her jewels, such evil-doers shall descend into the lower species."

"If a woman is not happy and dressed in a manner becoming her, she will not fill her husband's heart with joy; and if the husband is not joyful, the marriage will be sterile."

"When the woman is happy, the family is in like manner happy."

"The virtuous woman should have but one husband, as the right-minded man should have but one wife."

"Under the regime of the Vedas, marriage was held so

indissoluble, that even death could not restore either party to liberty, if children had been born of the union. The one remaining in exile upon earth, should live upon memories, and in mourning, until the day of death permitted re-union in the bosom of Brahmā with its other half, the holy affection which it had lost."

How grand in its moral sense was the idea of duty and honour, of this civilisation of early ages, which, so near the infancy of humanity, had not yet seen the rise of those baneful ambitions, which since, in partitioning the earth and strewing it with ruins, have made man forget his celestial origin, and the sacred innocence of his first existence.

Manifestly we cannot accept Judaism, with its train of superstitions, immoralities and atrocities, as the guardian of primitive revelation, and the inspirer of modern intelligence. **Judea, like Persia and Egypt, is a product of the decay of Vedic society; and has but gathered a few of the grand traditions of the mother-country, to mutilate and adapt them to the morals of the epoch.**

The first result of the baneful domination of priests in India, has the abasement and moral degradation of the woman, so respected and honoured during the Vedic period.

The sacerdotal caste in Egypt followed the inspiration of the Brāhmaṇas, and took care to make no change in that situation.

If you would reign over the persons of slaves, over brutalised intelligence, the history of these infamous epochs presents a means of unequalled simplicity: *Degrade and demoralise the woman,* and you will soon have made of man a debased creature, without energy to struggle against the darkest despotism; for according to the fine expression of the Vedas, **"the woman is the soul of humanity!"**

How perfectly did the mysterious and unknown author of the sacred books of India understand that the woman — daughter, wife and mother — held the family by the heart's most sacred ties, and that in inspiring the family with her gentle and chaste virtue, she moralised society.

But how well, too, did those corrupt priests, thirsting for power, understand that there was the joint, there the knot to be severed for more secure establishment of their dominion!

Did Moses come to change this state of things and to restore to woman her true role, that which she has before fulfilled in primitive times of the East?

No!

Did he concede to the morals of the epoch, against which he was powerless to contend? — Possibly, — but then it is only another reason for talking to us no more about revelation!

Ah! partisans of Jehovah, what a paltry idea you seek to give us of God — and on what curious traditions repose your beliefs!

What! here is a civilisation which you cannot deny to be older than your own, which places the woman on a level with the man, gives them an equal place in the family and in society; decay comes and reverses these principles. You appear and proudly call yourselves "the people of God," while you are only the rotten produce of Indian decomposition, incapable of recovering the pure doctrines of primitive ages, or of rehabilitating your mothers!

Avaunt, then, people of Israel — offspring of parias, cease preaching to us of your divine origin, — your reign was but one of violence and bloodshed; and you were incapable of comprehending woman, who alone could have regenerated you!

You have Ruth, it is true, of the candour and touching poetry of whose rele you boast. We know what she was worth, and how she prostituted herself to Boaz, by the advice of her mother, to make him marry her.

It was the usage of the times, you will rely, and that is precisely my reproach against you who profess yourselves the begotten of revelation.

Wherefore did you not change these usages? You knew how to construct the code of conquest by pillage, fire, and sword, but you were powerless to legislscandiskate for purity, propriety, and social morality.

Remember the daughters of Lot prostituting themselves to their father! Abraham casting out his own children by his maid-servants! Thamar delivering herself to her father-in-law!

Recollect that priest, the levite of Ephraim, who, to calm to fury of some drunken men and escape their violence, turned out his wife for their gratification, and abandoned her to a whole night of violation! It is time to appreciate all things at their true value! If you are not revelation. I accept your excuse, and admit with your that these vile abuses were the usages of time a revelation. I repudiate you, and I tell you that your revelation is immoral!

Oh! you would have us believe that God created a progressive and perfectible morality? That there is an old law tolerating, and a new law proscribing, immorality?

Well! I tell you in reply, that there is but one eternal moral law ordained by God at the cradle of humanity, and that all those peoples who have ignored it have violated the law of God.

A circumstance that has always astonished me is to see the branches of modern Protestantism, of that religion of free judgement, reject from their communion those whose faith in the light of reason denies revelation.

A man, called illustrious because he overthrew a throne, and who would overthrow many others but for that he is for the moment unemployed because of disqualifying ineptness, has lately devoted himself to preaching in books.

He is not a Catholic, for he has not that ardent holy faith that would excuse his Catholicism.

He is not a Protestant, for he proscribes independence and

freedom of thought. He is not a Jew, for he admits the ancient law for the past, and rejects if for the present.

Then what is he?

He was a man who disdained men, a minister who despised minister, a deputy who scorned electors, and a subject who contemned his king.

In short, he is a man, who, after freely despising each and all is now in a fair way to receive what he so liberally bestowed.

Well! this man, who has set about preaching in his books, has made himself the champion of Hebrew revelation.

He believes this, because it suits him; he rejects that, because it displeases him; he is eclectic, but it is of his own eclecticism; he is a freethinker, but of his own free thoughts, and he will have none other.

What impels him to this last proceeding?

The desire to surround his name with a final êclat. Come, M. Guizot, quit your pen, as you have quitted the ministry. All that I can tell you, on behalf of youthful thinkers, is, that you dishearten both believers and freethinkers. We may respect one who defends an idea or a standard (flag), but never those who have no other idea, or other flag then self.

I have just re-perused this entremet, which, perhaps, ought not to soil my pages — ought I to efface it? No! my pen may perchance have met a cry of public conscience.

The name presented itself among many defenders of Hebrew revelation, and was the only one that attracted me, because the only one that so impressively suggested the individual, the Ego (Moi), and personified social, political, and religious egotism in itself.

Let us suppose all this but a parenthesis, and return to our subject.

I have said to revelation, that it is not revelation because not constructed to rehabilitate woman, and because rejecting the traditions of ancient India, the India of the Vedas, it does but continue the traditions of Brahmanical times.

The woman of the Vedas is chaste and respectable, — the woman of the Bible is but a slave, and sometimes but a prostitute.

The woman of the Vedas is companion for man, and the honour of the domestic hearth. The woman of the Bible is but a concubine.

The Hindu could have but one wife.

The Israelite made excursions into neighbouring territories to procure himself virgins, and he did not hesitate to sell his own daughter when he found a good price.

It is not necessary to seek elsewhere then in the corruption of Hebrew morals, the motives which impelled Moses to change the parts, and mutilate the Indian version of creation, which he copied in Egypt from the sacred books of the priests.

The Hebrew legislator could not at this lawless epoch, introduce the beautiful and touching figure, — the woman, free, chaste and devoted, reigning in the hearts of her husband and her children. Let us admit, further, in his defence, that had he had the courage to make the attempt, — his people would not have understood it, and he would infallibly have sunk under a general revolt.

Throughout the East, woman had become the slave of a master, and none yet dreamt of emancipating and restoring her to her place; nor had Moses, more than others, an idea of reviving primitive traditions.

He could not then, in such circumstances, transcribe the Indian legend in all its sublime simplicity.

To have made man the author of original sin would have diminished the prestige and shocked the pride of the despot, and have made woman understand that she had been wrongfully disfranchised, in the name of the Divinity.

But it is not in this only that Moses forgot India; in Genesis Jehovah announces no redeemer to Adam and Eve, after their fault; and I confess it is not without astonishment that I see the Christian idea rely upon Moses, to maintain that the Lord announced the Messiah to our first parents.

See what says Genesis, when Adam is expelled from Paradise:"

And he (Jehovah) said, Behold Adam is become almost like one of us (Jehovah does not appear to me quite certain that he is the One and only God), knowing good and evil, he must now be expelled, lest he again raise his hand to the tree of life, and eating of its fruit, live eternally."

"God then turned him out of the garden of delight, that he might cultivate the earth, whence he was taken."

"And having expelled him, he placed cherubim before the garden of Paradise, with flaming swords to guard the tree of life.

"I have vainly examined each sentence, each expression, not only of this book, but also of the four others attributed to Moses, and have found it impossible to discover anything which, distinctly or indistinctly, plainly or figuratively, could possibly apply to a Redeemer.

It was but later that the prophets recovered this tradition which India had bequeathed to all the peoples, and which we find all the sacred books of the world.

It may be well, also, to remark, that Moses says not a word about the creation and revolt of the angels, which we regard as another posterior adoption from the traditions of the East.

Thus does this Hebrew religion from itself little by little, from parts and pieces, gathered here and there from all ancient mythologies, and placed under the guardianship of a revelation, which will not bear examination.

It results from all this, that Moses knew much less of the sacred books of India and of Egypt, than the Levites and prophets who afterwards completed his work.

VI

THE DELUGE, ACCORDING TO THE *MAHĀBHĀRATA* AND BRAHMANICAL TRADITION

Here we have but an *embarras de choix*: there is not a record of ancient India, treatise on theology, or poem, that fails to give its special version of the great cataclysm of which all peoples retain the tradition.

An abridged Vedic version of the event narrates that "According to the Lord's prediction, the earth became peopled, and the sons of *Ādima* and Heva grew so numerous and so wicked that they could no longer agree among themselves. They forgot God and his promises, and ended by wearying him with the clamour of their bloody quarrels.

"One day, King Daytha had even the audacity to launch his imprecations against heaven's thunder, commanding silence, and threatening in default, to conquer heaven at the head of his warriors."

"The Lord then resolved to inflict upon his creatures a terrible chastisement, which should serve as a warning to survivors and to their descendants.

"Thus we see Brahmā did not, like the Jehovah of the Bible exhibit the weakness inconsistent with his prescience of regretting that he had created the world.

Brahmā having cast his eyes over the world to discover the man who, of all others, deserved to be saved for the continuance of the human race, chose Vaivasvata, because of his virtues; and we here learn how he made known his will, and the results.

Vaivasvata had reached that period of life when ardent servants of God should withdraw from family and friends, and retire into forests and deserts, to end their days in the midst of austerities and in perpetual contemplation of the pure divine essence.

One day as he came to perform his ablution on the sacred banks of the Viriny, a little fish of most brilliant colours came and threw itself upon the sand, crying to the holy man, "Save me! if you do not listen to my prayer, I shall inevitably be devoured by the larger fish that inhabit the river.

"Moved with pity, Vaivasvata placed it in the brazen vase, which served him to dip water from the river, and carried it home, where it, Vaivasvata was obliged to transport it to a tank, where its growth continuing with the same rapidity, it be sought its preserver to convey it to the Ganges."That," answered the holy hermit, "is beyond my strength, one should be Brahmā's self now to withdraw you from where you are."

"At least try," replied the fish. "And Vaivasvata having seized it, with the greatest facility raised and conveyed it to the sacred river, and not only was this enormous fish as light as a straw, but it also effused about itself the sweetest perfumes.

Vaivasvata perceived that he was accomplishing the will of the Lord and was in expectation of wonderful events.

The fish soon recalled him, and this time demanded to be transported to the ocean, which was accomplished with the same promptness.

It then said to its preserver; "Listen, O wise and beneficent man: the globe is about to be submerged, and all that inhabit it shall perish, for behold the wrath of the Lord shall breathe upon the clouds and the seas, to charge them with the chastisement of this corrupt and wicked race, who forget their origin and the law of God. Your fellow creatures can no longer contain their pride, and even dare to defy their Creator, but their offences have reached the foot of Brahmā's throne, and Brahmā is about to make known his power."

"Hasten, then, to construct a vessel in which you shall embark yourself with all your family."

"You will take also seeds of every plant and a couple of each species of animals, leaving all such as are begotten of vapours and rottenness — for their principle of life does not emanate from the great Soul?

"And you will wait with confidence."

Vaivasvata hastened to obey these instruction, and, having constructed the ship, shut himself up with his family therein, with the seeds of plants and a couple of all animals, as has been said.

When the rain began to fall and the seas to overflow, a monstrous fish, armed with a gigantic horn, came and placed itself at the head of the ship, and Vaivasvata having attached a cable to the horn, the fish darted froth to conduct and guide the ship in the midst of all the unchained elements.

And those in the ship saw that the hand of God protected them, for the fury of the tempest or the violence of the waves harmed them not. This lasted for days and months and years, until the work of destruction was entirely completed. The elements having calmed, the navigators, always guided by their mysterious conductor, were able to land on the summit of the Himalayas.

"It is Viṣṇu that has saved you from death," said the fish on leaving them, "it is at his prayer that Brahmā has pardoned humanity — go now, re-people the earth and accomplish the work of God."

According to tradition, it was by reminding Brahmā that he had promised to send him upon earth to lead back men to the primitive faith and to redeem their transgressions, that Viṣṇu obtained the preservation of Vaivasvata, that the promise of God might be thereafter fulfilled.

This legend, we think, needs no commentary; and the reader will easily perceive all the consequent conclusions.

According to some, Vaivasvata was the father, through his progeny, of all new peoples.

According to others, he had but to throw pebbles into the mud left by the waters, to produce men in as great numbers as he desired.

On one side it is the myth, recovered and adopted by Judaism and the Christian dogma.

On the other it is the tradition of Deucalion and Pyrrha, brought to Greece in the poetic chants of emigrants.

VII

THE LEGEND OF THE PATRIARCH AJIGARTA

Obviously we cannot here enter upon a history of the descendants of Vaivasvata, nor relate all Indian legends that touch upon patriarchal life after the deluge. We shall confine ourselves to that of Ajigarta, which, from its striking resemblance to that a Abraham of the Bible, will signally support our proposition, that Moses obtained his traditions of Genesis, patriarchal and others, from the sacred books of Egypt, which were themselves but a rescript of the Vedas and religious beliefs of India, — a conclusion form which there is no escape, but by persistently judging those ancient epochs by the absurd fables of the Hebrew legislator, aided by a chronology, of which modern science has established the impossibility.

It is curious, in fact, in examining this chronology, to see the determination with which Moses attaches himself to Adam. I doubt the possibility of finding anything in the world more repulsive to the most common laws of common sense.

According to the Bible:

Moses was long a contemporary of Levi!

Levi lived thirty-one years with Isaac.

Isaac lived fifty years with Shem:

Shem lived ninety-six years with Mathusalem:

Mathusalem lived forty-three years with Adam:

Thus Moses would be only separated from the creatica of the world by four generations, and from the deluge, by two generations!

It is to be remarked that the four men who separated Moses from Adam would, according to biblical chronology, have lived two thousand four hundred and thirty-three years, or six hundred years for each life.

"So that the creation of the world, and all that is recorded in Genesis, might have become known to Moses through recitals personally made to him by his fathers. Perhaps even the memories yet existed amongst the Israelites, and from those recollection he may have recorded the dates of births and deaths of the patriarchs, the numbering of their children and their families, and the names of the different countries in which each became established under the guidance of the Holy Spirit, which we must always regard as the chief author of the sacred books.

"We must, however, understand each other, my reverend father!

Moses knew no trinity. I defy you to cite a single line of his work contradictory of this affirmation. Wherefore, then, substitute the Holy Spirit for Jehovah? You do not say, but I understand; it is by the aid of these adjunctions, for which you are never at a loss when needful, that you explain the Bible, and there discover what does not exist.

It was bad enough to make these men live five, six, seven, nine hundred years like Mathusalem, without taking the trouble to introduce the Holy Spirit, who ought, if respected, to have nothing in common with these gross traditions.

It must be confessed, however, that our history is easily contented since the twenty times triumphant refutations of science, she still persists in adopting this Hebrew chronology.

According to Indian chronology, the deluge occurred at the end of the *Dvāpara-Yuga*, that is the third age of the world's existence, more than four thousand years before our era, and in the following age lived Ajigarta, the grandson of Vaivasvata.

The following legend relates to this patriarch, who lived two thousand five hundred years before Moses, and who, no doubt, suggested to Moses the legend of Abraham:

"In the country of Ganges, lived a virtuous man of the name of Ajigarta; morning and evening he retired to woody glades, or to the banks of rivers whose waters are naturally pure, to offer sacrifice.

"And when the sacrifice was offered, and his mouth purified by Divine nourishment, after having softly pronounced the mysterious word — *Aum*! which is an appeal to God — he chanted the consecrated hymn of the *Sâvitri*:
> "*Bhur*!   *Bhuvah*!   *Svah* !

(Earth   Midspace.   Interstellar space)\

"Lord of the worlds and of all creatures, receive my humble invocations, turns from the contemplation of thy immortal power — Thy single glance shall purify my soul.

"Come to me, that I may hear thy voice in the fluttering of the leaves, in the murmuring waters of sacred river, in the sparkling flame of the Avasathya (consecrated fire).

My soul longs to breathe the air that emanates from the great Soul; Listen to my humble invocation. Lord of all words and of all creatures.

> "*Bhur*!   *Bhuvah*!   *Svah* !

(Earth   Midspace.   Interstellar space)

"Thy word shall be sweeter to my thirsty soul than the tears of night to the sandy desert, sweeter than the voice of the young mother who caresses her infant."

"Come to me, O thou by whom the earth blooms into flowers, by whom harvests ripen, by whom all germs develop themselves, by whom glitter the heavens, mothers produce children, and sages learn virtue."

"My soul thirsteth to know thee, and to escape from its mortal envelope to the enjoyment of celestial bliss, absorbed in thy splendour.

> "*Bhur*!   *Bhuvah*!   *Svah*!"

(Earth.   Midspace   Interstellar space)

"After this invocation to God, the sage Ajigarta turned himself towards the Sun, and to it, as the most magnificent creation of Brahmā, addressed this hymn:"

'O radiant and glorious Sun, accept the homage which I address to thine ever young and ever excellent attributes.

"Deign to accord my prayer, that thy rays may descend upon my hungry spirit, as a young lover hastens to receive the first kisses of his mistress.

"Sun! lustrous orb, that fertilizeth and rejoiceth both the earth and the sea! shine upon me."

"Pure and resplendent Sun, let us consider thine excellent light, that it may brighten and direct our intelligence. "The priests, by sacrifices and holy chants honour, thee, O resplendent Sun, for their intelligence discovers in thee the most beautiful work of God.

"Hungering for celestial food, I solicit by my humble prayers, thy divine and precious gifts, O sublime and glorious Sun!'

(Extract from the *Ṛgveda*)

"After reciting these prayers and making the prescribed ablutions, the sage Ajigarta still devoted the greater part of the day to study of the profound and mystic meaning of the Veda, under the direction of a holy person named Pāvaka, (the purified), who was not far from that age (seventy years) when the true servant of God should retire from the world to lead a life of seclusion."

"When Ajigarta had completed his forty-fifth year, having passed his days in study and prayer, his master, one morning when sacrifice was over, presented to him a heifer, without spot, and crowned with flowers, saying:

"Behold the gift which the Lord ordains for those who have completed the study of the Veda, you no more require my instructions, O Ajigarta; think now of procuring for yourself a son who may accomplish on your tomb the funeral ceremonies which should introduce you to the abode of Brahmā.'"

'Father,' replied Ajigarta, 'I hear your words, and understand the necessity; but I know not a woman, and if my heart desired to love, it knows not where to address its prayer.'

"I have given you life by the understanding,' said Pāvaka, 'I will now give you the life of happiness and love.

"My daughter Pārvati excel amongst all virgins for beauty and discretion, from her birth I have destined her for your wife — her eyes have not yet rested upon man, nor have a man beheld her gracious countenance."

"On hearing these words, Ajigarta was filled with joy."

"The wedding feast took place, and the marriage was consecrated after the manner of *dvijas*.

"Years slipped on with nothing to disturb the felicity of Ajigarta and the beautiful Pāravatī: their herds were the largest and best tended; their harvests of rice of small grains and of saffron, were always the finest. But one thing was wanting to their happiness: Pāravatī although her husband had always approached her at the favourable season, according to the law of God, had given him no child, and seemed struck with sterility."

"Vain her pilgrimage to the scared waters of the Ganges—vain her numberless vows and prayers; — she had not conceived."

"The eighth year of her sterility approached, when, according to the law, Pāravatī should be divorced as not having produced a son, — which was a subject of continued desolation to them both."

"When, one day, Ajigarta, took a young red goat, the finest of his herd, and went to a desert mountain to sacrifice it to God, as with flowing tears he prayed, 'Lord, separate not those whom thou hast united.' But sobs choked his voice, and he could, say no more."

"As he lay with his face to the earth, groaning and imploring God, a voice, which sounded from the clouds, made him tremble, and he distinctly heard these words:

— 'Return to thy house, Ajigarta, the Lord has heard thy prayer, and has had pity on thee.'

"As he returned towards home, his wife, full of joy, ran to meet him, and as for a long time he has not seen her joyful, he inquired the reason of her unusual satisfaction."

"During thine absence, replied Pāravatī, a man who appeared worn out with fatigue came to rest himself under the veranda of our house. I offered him the pure water, boiled rice and ghee which we give to strangers, — after having eaten, and when about to depart he said to me:— 'Thy heart is sad and thine eyes dimmed from tears; — rejoice thyself, for soon shalt thou conceive, and a son shall be born of thee whom thou shalt name Śunaḥśepa (the reward of Alms), who shall preserve to thee the love of thy husband, and be the honour of his race."

"And Ajigarta having in his turn recounted what had happened to him, they rejoiced together in their hearts, for they trusted that their ills were at an end, and that they would not be obliged to separate."

"Night having come, and Ajigarta, having perfumed him self, and well rubbed his limbs with saffron, approached Pāravatī, for she was at the propitious season, and she conceived."

"The day of the child's birth was celebrated with general rejoicing, in which relations, friends, and servants participated."

"Pāravatī alone did not assist, for he was dead to the world, and only lived in contemplation of the Lord."

"The child received the name of Śunaḥśepa, as it had been said."

"Pāravatī had afterward many daughters, who were the

ornaments of the house for their beauty, but God gave her not another son."

"As the child approached its twelfth year, and was distinguished above all for strength and shape, his father resolved to proceed with him to perform commemorative *yajña* on the mountain where the Lord had before granted his prayer.

"After having, as on the first occasion, selected a young goat, without, spot, and of a red fleece, from his herd, Ajigarta proceeded on his way with his son."

"Advancing on their way, through a thick forest, they came upon a young dove which had fallen from its nest, unfledged and pursued by a serpent; Śunaḥśepa darted upon the reptile, and having killed it with his staff, he replaced the young dove in its nest— and the mother, circling about his head, thanked him with her joyous cries."

"Ajigarta was delighted to see that his son was courageous and good."

"Having reached the mountain, they set about gathering wood for the *yajña*; but while so occupied the goat which they had tied to a tree broke its rope and fled."

"Then said Ajigarta, Behold here is wood for the pile, but we have no longer an oblation: and he knew not what to do, for they were far from any habitation; and yet he would not return without accomplishing his vow."

"'Return,' and said he to his son, 'to the nest where you replaced the young dove, and bring it to me; in default a goat, it will serve us as a oblation."

"Śunaḥśepa was about to obey the orders of his father, when the angry voice of Brahmā was heard, as it said:"

"Wherefore command your son to go in search of the dove which he saved, to immolate it in place of the goat which you have allowed to escape? Did you then only save it from the serpent to imitate its evil action? Such *yajña* would not be agreeable to me."

"'He who destroys the good that he has done is not worthy to address his prayers to me."

"'Behold the first fault that thou has committed, O Ajigarta! To efface it thou shalt immolate the son that I have given thee, on this pile — such is my will."

"On hearing these words Ajigarta was seized with profound anguish, he sat himself down upon the sands, and tears flowed abundantly from his eyes."

"'O Pāravatī,' he exclaimed, 'what wilt thou say, when thou shalt see me return alone to the house, and what can I answer when thou shalt demand of me what has become of thy first born?'

"And thus he bemoaned himself until the evening unable to resolve on accomplishing the *yajña*. Nevertheless he dreamt not of disobeying the Lord, and Śunaḥśepa, notwithstanding his tender age, was firm, and encouraged him to execute the divine commands."

"Having gathered the wood and constructed the pile, with a trembling hand he bound his son, and, raising his arm with the knife of *yajña*, was about to cut his throat, when Viṣṇu, in the form of a dove, came and sat upon the head of the child."

"'O Ajigarta,' said he, 'cut the victim's bands and scatter the pile; God is satisfied of thy son by his courage hath found grace before him. Let the days of his life be long, for it is from him that shall be born the virgin who shall conceive by a divine germ!'

"Ajigarta and his son offered long thanks givings to the Lord; then, the night having come, they retraced their home ward way, discoursing of these wonderful things, and full of confidence in the goodness of the Lord," (Ramatsariar, Prophecies).

The two hymns to Brahmā and to the Sun are hot round in the legend, which confines itself to recording the prayers of

Ajigarta on the mountain. The reader will, however, approve of our having extracted them from the *Ṛgveda*, and *Sāmaveda*, for this translation. Such is the antique memoir of the *yajña*, of Ajigarta, which, on our first acquaintance with it, filled us with profound astonishment.

We are indebted to the great Orientalist, William Jones, for the first trace of its existence. In reading, one day, his translation of Manu, a note led us to consult the Hindu commentator, Kulluka Bhaṭṭa, where we found allusion to this sacrifice of the son by the father, which God arrested, after having himself commanded it. Thenceforth it became our fixed idea to recover from the inextricable pages of Hindu religious books the original record of this event, in which success would have been to us impossible, but for the complaisance of a Brahmin, with whom we were studying Sanskrit, and who, in concession to our prayer, produced to us from the library of his pagoda, the works of the theologian Ramatsariar, which have been to us so precious a support in the preparation of this volume.

"When such proofs thus accord with the aggregate, would it not be against evidence to resist the conclusion that all ancient traditions had a common origin, of which the substructure should be sought in the myths of India?

I cannot too often repeat, that if it be true and logical to say that all modern peoples have quaffed from the same source of philosophic and religious light, then how can it be illogical to maintain that all the peoples of antiquity did but adopt, under modifications, the beliefs of their predecessors? This legend of the patriarch Ajigarta, manipulated by Moses became the legend of Abraham.

VIII

INCARNATIONS — PROPHECIES ANNOUNCING THE COMING OF CHRISTNA (KRISHNA)

We shall enlighten nobody, probably, in announcing that the incarnation, that is to say, the descent of God upon earth to regenerate his creatures, is the base of the Indian religion. That is sufficiently known to all who have ever opened a book upon India, to place us perfectly at ease in vindicating that country's priority in this religious belief.

"But if the truth seem generally admitted, if no one contests that India has had her incarnation, there has hitherto appeared no other disposition than to ridicule these traditions, and absolutely to represent the different *Avataras* of Brahmā among men as senseless superstitions.

"It would be easy for us to discover the source of these opinions, which could not be impartial, emanating as they did from missionaries of all these forms of worship, who found themselves in competitive antagonism in India with beliefs similar to those they came to preach.

For this purpose they adopted the very means we describe; instead of studying the religious principles of the Hindus in their special books of theology, where they might have found — not wars, but sublime instructions, they addressed themselves to poetry, fable and heroic traditions, to enable them at their case to mock at Brahmā, at incarnations, and at trinities.

"A Hindu priest might play precisely the same role in Europe if rejecting Gospel *morale*, and the sublime lessons of Christ, he persisted, designedly, in studying our religion only in the sacred dramas and religious farces of the Middle Ages, where God the Father comes upon the stage to take the devil by the throat; where they assign to the Virgin, to Jesus, to apostles, and to saints, absurdities the most sacrilegious, and sometimes even obscene!

In the East, the region of dreams and of poetry, religion should be studied much less than elsewhere in works of imagination, which multiply to infinity, angels, saints, and demons, and introduce them constantly in the operations of God and the actions of men.

We must study with Brahmin priests, and study their books, and smile with them at all the superstitions that Europe assigns to India, and at the interested report of a few interested men.

According to Hindu belief, there have up to this time been nine *Avataras* of God upon earth: The first eight were but short apparitions of Divinity, coming to renew to holy individuals, the promise of Redeemer made to Adam and Héva after their fall; — the ninth alone is an incarnation, that is to say, a realisation of the prediction of Brahmā. This incarnation is that of Christna, (Krishna), son of the Devakī.

Here are some of the predictions which announce his coming, collected by Ramatsariar, in Atharva, the *Vedāṅga* and the *Vedanta*. The *Vedānta* announce that the incarnation of Christna (Krishna) should occur in the early times of the *Kaliyuga*, that is, of the actual age of the world. This expression, we think, calls for an explanation.

The Indians divide the time of the world's duration into four ages, which should renew themselves by four different revivals before the *Mahāpralaya*, or general destruction of all that exists.

The first is known as the *Kṛta yuga*, and has a duration of one million seven hundred and twenty-eight thousand human years of three hundred and sixty days.

The second is named *Tretā yuga* and has a duration of one million two hundred and ninety-six thousand human years.

The third, called *Dvāpara yuga*, has a duration of eight

hundred and sixty-four thousand human years.

Lastly, the fourth, of four hundred and thirty-two thousand year's duration, is called the *Kaliyuga*.

Of this last, the actual age of the world, about four thousand five hundred years have now elapsed.

Sir William Jones, in his Asiatic studies, does not doubt that the Greek and Roman division of time into four ages — the golden age, the silver age, the brazen age, and the iron age, is but a souvenir of Indian tradition— another testimony in favour of our views of the origin of those peoples.

IX

BIRTH OF DEVAKĪ

We have now arrived at this marvellous Indian incarnation — the first in date among all the religious incarnations of our globe — the first equally to recall to men those eternal truths impressed by God on human conscience, and which are too often obscured by the strifes of despotism and intolerance.

We shall simply describe, according to the most incontestable Indian authorities, the life of the Devakī, and that of her divine son, reserving for the present, all comment and comparison.

The sister of the Rājā, mother of the infant, some days before her accouchement, had a dream, in which Viṣṇu, appearing to her in all the eclat of his splendour, came to reveal to her the future destinies of the expected child.

"Thou shalt call the infant, Devakī-guy, said he to the mother," for it is through her that the designs of God should be accomplished. Let no animal food ever approach her lips — rice, honey, and milk should be her only sustenance. The little girl at her birth received the name of Devakī as had been commanded; and her mother, fearing that in the palace of her brother, who was a wicked man, she might not be able to fulfil the prescription of God, conveyed her to the house of one of her relatives, named Nanda, lord of the small village on the banks of the Yamuna, and celebrated for his virtues. Her brother, to whom she announced her departure or pilgrimage to the sacred river, fearing the murmurs of the people, dared not oppose her designs.

Nevertheless, to show his discontent, he but allowed her a most mediocre escort; consisting only of two elephants, which would scarcely have been sufficient for a woman of low extraction.

Towards evening, scarcely had Lakṣmī commenced her march, when a suite, composed of more than a hundred elephants, caparisoned in gold, and conducted by men sumptuously clothed, joined her; and as night came, a column of a fire appeared in the air to guide them, to the sound of mysterious music that seemed to come from heaven.

And all those who assisted at this marvellous departure understood that it was not ordinary, and that the mother and the infant were protected by the Lord.

The Rājā of Mathura became exceedingly jealous, and urged by the prince of the Rākṣasas, who desired to thwart the views of Viṣnu, sent by a side road, armed men to disperse the escort and bring back his sister to his palace.

He would then have said— "You see the roads are not safe, and you cannot hope to make so long a journey without danger; send a holy hermit in your place, and he will accomplish your vow.

"But scarcely had the soldiers whom he had sent, come in sight of the escort of Lakṣamī, when, enlightened by the Spirit of God, they joined themselves to it, to protect the mother and infant en route.

"And the Rājā became furious on hearing of the failure of his evil action. The same night it was made known to him a dream, that of Devakī should be born a son, who should dethrone and chastise him for all his crimes.

He then thought to conceal his dark projects in his heart, assured that later he would easily succeed in enticing his niece to his court, should his sister refuse to return to him, and that it would be possible for him to effect her death, and escape that fate with which he was menaced.

The better to conceal his design, he sent messengers loaded with many present to be conveyed to Yaśodā, for presentation to their relation Nanda.

The journey of Lakṣmī to the banks of the Ganges was but

a triumphal march; from all sides the population crowded her passage, saying amongst themselves — " What queen is this who possesses such a splendid escort, this must be the wife of the most powerful prince of the earth." And from all parts they bought her flowers to strew the way, and fruits and rich presents.

But what most astonished the crowd was the beauty of the young Devakī, who, although but a few days old, had already the serious countenance of a woman, seeming to understand what passed around her and the admiration of which she was the object.

During the journey, which lasted sixty days, the column of fire, invisible with the sun, reappeared at night, and never ceased to direct the cortége until its arrival. And, most wonderful — the tigers, panthers, and wild elephants, far from flying, as usual, with terror at the approach of man, came gently to observe the suite of Lakṣmī; and their howlings became as tender as the songs of nightingales, that they might not frighten the infant. Nanda, informed of the arrival of his relative, by a messenger from Viṣṇu, came two days' march from his habitation to meet her, followed by all his servants, and the moment he perceived Devakī — he saluted her by the name of mother' saying to all those who were astonished at the word, "she will be mother to us all, for of her will be born the Spirit that shall regenerate us."

X

INFANCY OF DEVAKĪ — DEATH OF HER MOTHER — HER RETURN TO MATHURA

The first years of Devakī glided on in peace in the house of Nanda, and without the least attempt by the tyrant of Mathura to entice her to him. On the contrary, he seized every occasion to send her presents, and to thank Nanda for the hospitality which he had extended to Lakṣmī and her daughter, which led all the believe that the light of the Lord had touched him, and that he had become good.

In the meantime the young virgin grew up midst her companions, surpassing them all in discretion and beauty. None better than she, although scarce six years of age, knew how to conduct the duties of the house, to spin flax or wool, and to diffuse joy and prosperity throughout the family.

Her happiness was in solitude — lost in the contemplation of God, who showered upon her all his blessings, and often afforded her celestial presentiment of what should happen to her.

One day as she was performing her ablutions on the bank of the Yamunā, midst a crowd of another women who had come for the same purpose, a gigantic bird came sailing over her, and gently descending, deposited upon her head a crown of lotus flowers.

All the people were amazed, and imagined that this child was destined for great things.

Meanwhile occurred the death of Lakṣmī, after a short illness and Devakī learned in a dream that her mother had seen the gates of the blest abode of Brahmā open themselves before her, because her life had always been pure and chaste, and it was not necessary to perform the usual funeral ceremonies on her tomb.

Devakī, whose person was on earth, but whose thoughts were in heaven, did not weep, nor wear mourning for her mother as customary, for, as it is taught in the sacred books, she regarded death *as a birth unto the new life.*

Having heard of the misfortune that had fallen upon his niece, the tyrant of Mathura judged the moment propitious for the execution of his treacherous designs, and sent ambassadors to Nanda with many presents, praying restoration of the young Devakī to himself, as her nearest relative, since the death of her mother.

Nanda was profoundly grieved at this proposition, for he loved the child equally with his own, and could not divest himself of forebodings that gave a darkening aspect to the future of Devakī at the court of her uncle.

Yet the request being just, he left the young girl free to accept or to reject it.

Devakī, who knew that destiny called her to Mathura accompanied the ambassadors sent by her uncle, after invoking all God's blessings upon the house she was leaving.

"Remember," said Nanda, "that we shall be happy to see you again, should misfortune bring you back to us.

"The forebodings of her protector had not deceived him Scarcely was Devakī in the power of her uncle, when he, throwing off the mask, had her confined in a lower, of which he commanded the door to be walled up, to preclude the possibility of escape.

But the virgin was not distressed. She had already long received from heaven the knowledge of what should happen to her, and, full of confidence, she waited the moment fixed by God for accomplishing his celestial designs.

Yet the tyrant of Mathura was not undisturbed: a frightful famine desolated his states. Death had robbed him, one by one, of all his children, and he lived in constant fear of the most dismal catastrophes.

Pursued by the idea, suggested by his dream of long before, that he was to be dethroned by a son of Devakī, instead of repenting many crimes he had committed, and for which he had been already so severely chastised by the Lord, he resolved to relive himself of all apprehension on this subject by destroying his niece. For this purpose he had poison — extract of the most dangerous plants— mixed with the water and food passed each day to Devakī in her prison; but he was filled with alarm at the extraordinary fact — not only did the young girl not die, but she even seemed not to have perceived the poison.

He then left her without food, thinking that starvation might be more powerful than poison.

It was vain; Devakī continued to enjoy the most perfect health, and, despite the most active vigilance, it was impossible to know if she received food form some mysterious hand, or if the spirit of God alone sufficed for her support.

Seeing this, the tyrant of Mathura abandoned the idea of putting her to death, and was content to surround her prison with a strong guard, threatening his soldiers with the most fearful punishment if Devakī should elude their vigilance and escape.

But it was in vain; all these precautions could not obstruct fulfilment of the prophecy of Paulastya;

"The divine spirit of Viṣnu passed through the walls to join himself to his well-beloved."

XI

BIRTH OF KRISHNA — PERSECUTION OF THE TYRANT OF MATHURA— MASSACRE OF ALL THE MALE CHILDREN BORN IN THE SAME NIGHT AS KRISHNA

(According to the Bhāgavata and Brahmanical tradition), One evening, as the Devakī was praying, her ears were suddenly charmed with celestial music, her prison became illuminated and Viṣṇu appeared to her in all the êclat of his divine Majesty. Devakī fell in a profound ecstasy, and having been *overshadowed* (is the Sanskrit expression) by the spirit of God that desired to incarnate itself she conceived.

The period of her gestation was to her a time of continued enchantment; the divine infant afforded his mother infinite enjoyments, which made her forget earth, her captivity, and even her existence.

The night of Devakī's accouchement, and as the newly born uttered its first wail, a violent wind opened a passage through the walls of the prison, and Devakī was conducted with her son, by a messenger from Viṣṇu to a sheep-fold belonging to Nanda, situated on the confines of the territory of Mathura. The Newly-born was named Krishna (in Sanskrit, sacred). The shepherds, informed of the charge which was confided to them, prostrated themselves before the infant, and adored him. The same night, Nanda, inspired by God in dream, knew what had happened, and commenced his march, with his servants, and many other holy people, in search of Devakī and her son, to withdraw her from the intrigues of the tyrant of Mathura.

He, on hearing of the accouchement and wonderful escape of his niece, fell into an ungovernable rage; instead of understanding that it was useless to strive against the Lord, and demanding grace, he resolved, by every possible means, to pursue the son of Devakī, and to him to death, hoping thus to escape the fate with which he was menaced.

Having had another dream, warning him more precisely of the chastisement that awaited him, he, ordained the massacre in all his states, of all the children of the male sex, born during the night of the birth of Krishna, thinking thus surely to reach him who in his thought should drive him from his throne.

Guided, no doubt, by the inspiration of cunning Rākṣasas who desired to oppose the designs of Viṣṇu, a troop of soldiers reached the sheep-fold of Nanda, and as he had not yet arrived his servants were about to arm themselves to defend Devakī and her son, when all at once, O prodigy! the child who was at his mother's breast, began suddenly to grow,— in a few seconds he had attained the size of a child to ten years of age, and ran to amuse himself midst the herd of sheep.

The soldiers passed near him without suspicion, and not finding in the farm any child of the age of him whom they sought, returned to the city, dreading the rage, at their failure, of him who had sent them.

Shortly after arrived Nanda with all his troops, and his first care, was to prostrate himself, with all the holy persons who accompanied him, before Devakī and her divine child. Not considering them in a place of safety, he conducted them to the vans of the Yamuna and thus was Devakī enabled once more to behold the abodes of her infancy.

We shall not here transcribe the many details that refer to the first year of Krishna, they were passed in the midst of dangers without number, devised by those who had an interest in his death, but he always came out victorious from these contests, whether with men or with demons.

The poets who have exercised their imaginations on all these things, have so surrounded them with miracles, and with wonderful events, that a dozen volumes would scarce suffice to recount them.

Yet there is one fact of the God-Man which we cannot pass over in silence, because Jesuits in India have made use of it, and still do so every day to maintain that Krishna was of dissolute morals, and gave many examples of impurity.

One day, walking on the bank of Yamuna, Krishna perceived some fifty young girl who had completely stripped themselves for their ablution, and some of them, in this condition, were laughing and romping without thinking whether or not they might be seen by passers-by.

The child remonstrated with them, telling that it was not decent; they began to laugh and to throw water in his face.

Seeing which, Krishna by a gesture, sent all their clothes, scattered on the sands, to the top of a tamarind tree, thus making it impossible for them to dress themselves on coming out of the water.

Perceiving then their fault, the young girls implored pardon, which was accorded on condition of the promise which they made ever after to wear a veil when they came to the sacred river to make their ablutions.

The Jesuits have seized upon this legend, recounting it after their own fashion, and making it appear that Krishna had but removed the clothes of the young girls, to see them more at his leisure in their nudity.

This version is consistent with their programme, and need not surprise us. Not permitted to acknowledge Krishna they combat him with their usual weapons, and we know how clever they are at altering texts, and at seeing what nobody else has ever been able to find.

Have we not seen them attempting to garble certain chapters of modern history? What wonder if the same spirit presides in the Oriental missions?

XII

PREACHING OF KRISHNA

At the age of scarce sixteen, Christna (Krishna) quitted his mother and his relative Nanda, to perambulate India in preaching the new doctrine.

In this second period of his life, Hindu poetry represents him as in constant strife against the perverse spirit, not only of the people, but also of princes; he surmounts extraordinary dangers; contends, single-handed, against whole armies sent to destroy him; strews his way with miracles, resuscitating the dead, healing lepers, restoring the deaf and the blind, everywhere supporting the weak against the strong, the oppressed against the powerful, and loudly proclaiming to all, that he is the second person of the trinity, that is, Viṣṇu, come upon earth to redeem man from original transgression, to eject the spirit of evil, and to restore the reign of good.

And the populations crowded his way, eager, for his sublime instruction, and they adored him as a God, saying, "This is in deed the redeemer promised to our fathers!

"We put aside the miraculous events of the life of this reformer, which, like all the acts for that matter assigned to different prophets, who, at different epochs, have appeared on earth, seem to us to belong only to legend.

I believe no more in Krishna, God and worker of miracles, that I believe in other incarnations or other messengers of the Supreme Being who call themselves Buddha or Zoroaster, Manu or Moses, Christ or Mohammed. But I believe in Krishna, as a philosopher and moralist, I admire his lessons, so sublime and so pure, that, later, the founder of Christianity in Europe perceived that he could not do better than imitate them.

After some years of preaching, the Hindu reformer felt the necessity of surrounding himself with earnest and courageous disciples to whom he might delegate the duty of continuing his work, after having initiated them in his doctrines.

Amongst those who had for some time most assiduously followed him in his peregrinations, he distinguished Arjuna, a young man of one of the chief families of Mathura, and who had left all to attach himself to him; he confided to him his projects and Arjuna swore to devote life to his service and to the propagation of his ideas.

Gradually they were joined by a small troop of the faithful, who participated in their fatigues, their labours and their faith.

They led a life of hardship, and we understand that the equalising precepts or Krishna, his example, and the purity of his life had wakened the people from their lethargy; a spark of reviving vitality began to circulate throughout India, and the partisans of the past, as well as the rajahs, urged on by the tyrant of Mathura, ceased not to lay snares for them, and to persecute them, for they felt their power and their thrones tremble before the rising popular wave.

But nothing succeeded with them: it appeared as if a power more potent than them all, had determined to frustrate their designs, and to protect the proscripts.

Sometimes whole villages rose and chased the soldiers sent to arrest Krishna and his disciples; sometimes the soldiers themselves, moved and persuaded by the divine word of the prophet, threw away their arms and besought his pardon.

One day, even a chief of the troops sent against the reformer, and who had sworn to withstand both fear and persuasion, having surprised Krishna in an isolated place, was so struck with his majestic bearing that he stripped himself of his symbols of command, and entreated to be admitted into the number of the faithful. His prayer was granted and from that moment the new faith had no more ardent disciple and defender than himself.

His name was Sāravasta.

Often Krishna disappeared from the midst of his disciples, leaving them alone, as if to prove them in the most difficult moments, suddenly re-appearing amongst them to restore their sinking courage and to withdraw them from danger.

During these absences Arjuna governed the little community, and took the master's place at *Yajña* and prayer, and submitted without murmur to his commands.

But, as we have already said, the actions of Krishna's life are less important to us than a knowledge of his precepts and his *morale*.

He came not to found a new religion, for God could not destroy what He had once for all declared good, and revealed; his object was but to purify the old from all turpitudes, all the impurities, which from many ages the perverseness of men had gradually introduced, and he succeeded, despite all the hatreds and all the antagonism of champions of the past.

At his death the entire of India had adopted his doctrine and his principles; a faith, vivid, young, and fertile in results, had permeated all classes, their morale was purified, and the vanquished spirit of evil had been obliged to take refuge in his sombre abode — the regeneration promised by Brahmā was accomplished.

The teaching of Krishna was familiar and simple when addressed to the people, elevated and philosophic in communion with his disciples; it is in the double view that we are about to consider him.

XIII

KRISHNA'S LESSONS TO THE PEOPLE

Parable plays a large part in the familiar instruction of the Indian redeemer. Krishna preferred this symbolic form when addressing himself to the people, who could less readily comprehend his philosophic lessons on the immortality of the soul and of future life.

This manner of appealing to the intelligence and evoking the moral idea from the action of certain persons introduced for the purpose, is conformable to Oriental habits, and we know that table and allegory are the produce of Asiatic literature.

Nothing, we think, will render the popular labours, of Krishna more comprehensible than citation of one of his most celebrated parables, that of the fisherman, which is held in such high respect and honour in India, as to be carefully impressed upon the memories of children from the most tender age.

Krishna was returning from a distant expedition, and re-entering Mathura with his disciples. The inhabitants flocked in crowds to meet him and to strew his way with branches.

At some leagues from the city the people halted, demanding to hear the holy word; Krishna mounted a little eminence that overlooked the crowd, and thus began:

The Parable of the Fisherman.

"On the banks of the Yamuna, above the place where its sacred course divides itself into a hundred arms, lived a poor fisherman of the name of Durga.

"At dawn he proceeded to the river to make his ablutions after the manner prescribed by the holy books; and holding in his hand a freshly cut sprig of the divine herb, Kuśā, he piously repeated the prayer of the Sāvitrī, preceded by the three mysterious words: *Bhur, Bhavaḥ Svaḥ* (Earth, Midspace, Inter stellar space): then, soul and body thus purified, he went courageously to work to supply the wants of his large family.

"The Lord had given him by his wife, whom he had married at the age of twelve years, in all the flower of her virgin beauty, six sons and four daughters, who were his joy, for they were pious and good like himself.

"His eldest son was already able to assist him in conducting his boat and casting his nets, and his daughters, confined to the interior of the house, wove the long and silky hairs of the goat to make vestments, and pounded for their repast, the ginger, the coriander, and the saffron, for a paste, which, mixed with the juice of red pepper, should serve to dress the fish.

"In spite of continued labour, the family was poor' for, jealous of his honesty and his virtues, the other fishers had combined against Durga, and pursued him with their daily ill treatment."

"Now they deranged his nets, or during the night drew his boat up into the sands, that he might lose the whole next day in restoring it to the water."

"Again, when on his way to the city to sell the produce of his fishing, they would snatch his fish from him by force, or throw them into the dust, that, seeing them thus soiled nobody might buy them."

"Very often Durga returned in sadness to his hut, thinking that ere long he would be unable to provide for the wants of his family. Nevertheless, he failed not to present the finest fish he caught to saintly hermits, and received all the miserable who came knocking at his door, sheltered them under his roof, and shared with them the little he possessed, which was a constant subject of derision and mockery for his enemies, who directed all the beggars they met to him, saying to them, 'Go, and find Durga, he is disguised prince, who only fishes from caprice."

"And thus did they ridicule the misery which was their own work."

"But the times became very hard for all the world: a frightful famine desolated the whole country, rice and smaller grains having completely failed at the last harvest. The fishers, enemies of Durga, were very soon as miserable as himself, and, in their common misfortune, no longer thought of tormenting him.

"One evening, as the poor man returned from the Yamuna without having caught the smallest fish, remembering bitterly that nothing remained in his hut, he found a little child at the foot of tamarind tree, weeping and calling for its mother. Durga demanded of it whence it came, and who had thus abandoned it.

"The child replied that its mother had left it there, saying she was going to seek it something to eat.

"Moved with pity, Durga took the poor little one in his arms, and conveyed it to his house; his wife, who was good and kind, said he had done well not to leave it to die of hunger.

"But here was no ore rice, nor smoked fish; the curry stone had not resounded that evening in the hands of the young girls who strike it in cadence.

"The moon rose silently in the celestial concave; the whole family assemble for the evening invocation.

"All at once the little child began to sing:

"The fruit of the cataca purifies water, so good actions purify the soul, Take your nets, Durga, your boat floats on the Yamuna, and the fish await.

"'This is the thirteenth night of the moon, the shadow of the elephant falls to the east; the manes of ancestors demand honey, clarified butter, and boiled rice; the offering must be presented. Take thy nets, Durga thy boat is on the Yamuna and the fish attend."

'Thou shalt give a feast to the poor, where nectar shall flow as abundantly as the waters of the sacred river. Thou shalt offer to the Rudras, and the Ādityas (deceased ancestors), the flesh of red-fleeced goat, for the times of trial are completed. Take thy nets, Durga, thirteen times shalt thou cast them; thy bark floats on the Yamuna, and the fish await.

"Durga, amazed, thought it a notice sent him from above — he took his nest, and, with the strongest of his sons, descended to the water's edge.

"The child followed them, entered the boat with them, and, having taken an oar, directed their course."

"Thirteen times were the nets cast into the water, and at each cast the boat, bending under the weight and the number of fish, was obliged to return and lighten itself of its load on the shore. And the last time the infant disappeared.

"Full of joy, Durga hastened to relieve the hunger of his children; then, immediately remembering that there were other sufferings to soothe, he ran to his neighbours, the fishermen, forgetting the evil he had received from them, to share with them his abundance.

"These flocked in crowds, not daring to believe in such generosity, and Durga, on the spot, distributed amongst than the remains of his miraculous capture.

"During the whole time of the famine, Durga continued not only to feed his old enemies, but also to receive all the unhappy who crowded about him. He had but to cast his nets into the river, to obtain immediately all the fish he could desire.

"The famine over, the hand of God continued to protect him; and he became at last so rich, that he was able alone to build a temple to Brahmā of such sumptuous magnificence; that pilgrims from all parts of the globe came in crowds to visit it and to offer their devotions.

"And it is thus, inhabitants of Mathura, that you should protect weakness, aid each other, and never remember the offences of an enemy in his misfortune.

"Let us now at hazard, gather a few from the abundant legacy of maxims with which it was his pleasure to sprinkle his familiar instructions.

"The wrongs we inflict upon our neighbours, follow us like our shadow."

"The knowledge of man is but vanity, all his best actions are illusory, when he knows not to ascribe them to God."

"Love of his fellow-creature should be the ruling principle of the just man in all his works, for such weigh most in the celestial balance."

"He who is humble in heart and in spirit, is loved of God; he has need of nothing more."

"As the body is strengthened by muscles, the soul is fortified by virtue."

"There is no greater sinner than he who covets the wife of his neighbour.

"We call attention to the following maxim, which many believed to be of only yesterday;

"As the earth supports those who trample it under foot, and rend its bosom with the plough, so should we return good for evil"

"If you frequent the society of the good, your example is useless, fear not to dwell amidst the wicked for their conversion."

"If one inhabitant can cause the ruin of a whole village he should be expelled; if a village can ruin a whole district, it should be destroyed; but if a district occasioned loss of the soul, it should be abandoned."

"Whatever services we render to perverse spirits, the good we do them resembles characters written upon water, which are effaced as we trace them. But the good should be done for its own sake, for it is not on earth we should expect reward."

"When we die our riches remain behind; our relatives and our friends only follow us to the tomb; but our virtues and our vices, our good actions and our faults, follow us in the other life."

"The virtuous man is like the gigantic Banyan tree, whose beneficent shade, affords freshness and life to the plants that surround it."

"Science is useless to a man without judgement, as a mirror to a blind man."

"The man who only appreciates means, according as they conduce to his success, soon loses his perception of the just, and of sound doctrines.

"(For you, gentlemen, casuists, inventors of the maxim, 'the end justifies the means').

"The infinite and the boundless can alone comprehend the boundless and the infinite, God only can comprehend God."

"The honest man should fall before the blows of the wicked as the sandal-tree that, felled by the woodsman's stroke, perfumes the axe that wounds it.

"Listen now to the counsels of Krishna to the just man who would sanctify himself in the lord and merit eternal recompense.

"Let him devote himself each day to all the practices of pious devotion, and submit his body to the to the most meritorious austerities."

"Let him fear all worldly honour worse than poison, and feel only contempt for this world's riches.

"Let him well know that what is above all, is the respect of himself and the love of his fellow creatures.

"Let him abstain from anger, and from all evil treatment, even towards animals, whom we ought to respect in the imperfection that God has assigned them.

"Let him chase away sensual desires, envy and cupidity.

"Let him refrain from the dance, the song, music, fermented drinks, and gambling.

"Let him never be guilty of evil-speaking, calumnies, or impostures.

"Let him never look at women with love, and abstain from embracing them.

"Let him have no quarrels. "Let his house, his diet, and his clothes by always of the plainest.

"Let his right hand be always open to the poor and the unhappy, and let him never boast his benefits.

"When a poor man shall knock at his door, let him receive him, refresh him by washing his feet, serve him himself, and eat what remains, for the poor are the chosen of the Lord.

"But, above all, let him refrain through the whole course of his life from, in whatever way, molesting others; protect, love, and assist his fellow-creatures, thence flow the virtues most agreeable to God.

It is thus that Krishna diffused amongst this people healthy doctrines of the *morale,* thus that he initiated his auditors in the grand principles of charity, of abnegation, and of self-respect, at an epoch when the desert countries of the West were still only occupied by the savage hordes of the forests.

What, then, has our civilisation, so proud of its progress and its enlightenment, what has it added to these sublime lessons?

XIV

KRISHNA'S PHILOSOPHIC TEACHINGS

It is necessary to read in the Sanskrit text itself, and especially in the Bhagavad-Gitā, the sublime discourses of Krishna with his disciples, and particularly with Arjuna, to comprehend that the enlightenment which has been reflected even to us, had there long existed in the East.

Problems of the most lofty philosophy, a morale the most pure, the immortality of the soul, the future destinies of the a man who shall have lived according to the law of God; all are treated of in these sublime monologues, where the auditor's role is only to give replies, and thus afford the professor an opening for new lessons.

In our inability to give, within our confined space, the development becoming these great subjects, we shall confine our slaves to reproduction of the discourse of Krishna on the immortality of the soul; it will suffice to judge the others.

Arjuna:

Canst thou not tell us, O Krishna, what is that pure fluid which we have received from the Lord, and which must return to Him again?

Krishna:

The soul is the principle of life which Sovereign Wisdom employed to animate bodies, matter is inert and perishable, the soul thinks and acts, and it is immortal. Of thought is born will, and of the will is born action. Thence it is that man is the most perfect of terrestrial creatures, for he operates freely in intellectual nature, knowing to distinguish the true from the false, the just from the unjust, good from evil.

That inward knowledge, that will which conveys itself by the judgement towards what it likes, and withdraws itself from what it dislikes, renders the soul responsible for its action, responsible for its choice, and for this cause has God established rewards and punishments.

When the soul follows the eternal and pure light that guides it, naturally it is inclined to the good.

Evil, on the contrary, triumphs when it forgets its origin, and submits to be governed by exterior influences.

The soul is immortal, and must return into the Great Soul from which it issued; but as it was given to man pure from all stain, it cannot re-ascend to the celestial abode until it shall have been purified from all the faults committed through its union with matter.

Arjuna:

How is this purification effected?

Krishna:

The soul is purified by a shorter or longer course, according to its faults, in the infernal heavens (hell), the exclusion imposed upon it from re-union with the Great Whole, is the greatest infliction that it can feel, for its desire is to return to the primitive source and to merge itself into the soul of all that exists.

Arjuna:

Whence comes the imperfection of the human soul, which is a portion of the Great Soul?

Krishna:

The soul is not imperfect in its pure essence, the light of this sublime *ahaṁkāra* does not draw its obscurity from itself; if there existed in the nature of the soul a germ of imperfection, nothing could destroy it, and this germ developing itself, the soul would be perishable and mortal as well as the body. From its union with matter alone comes its imperfection, but that imperfection does not affect its essence, for it is not its cause, which is the supreme intelligence, which is God.

We must, here, is spite of ourselves, arrest this citation. Its continuation affords Krishna occasion to rise into regions of the most subtle metaphysics, and his reasoning would not, we think, be perfectly understood, except by people who had devoted their lives to the particular study and explored the depths of philosophic sciences.

Moreover, this simple glance suffices completely to elucidate the conclusions which we profess to draw from the work of the Indian reformer. To epitomise:

Krishna was born in India to preach the immortality of the soul, free will, that is to say, freedom of thought and liberty of person, belief in merit and demerit, in reward and punishment in the life of the future. He came to teach the people charity, love of each other, self-respect, the practice of good *for its own sake,* and faith in the inexhaustible good-will of the Creator.

He proscribed revenge commanded to return good for evil, consoled the feeble, sustained the unhappy and the oppressed, denounced tyranny.

He lived poor and loved the poor. He lived chaste and prescribed chastity.

He was, we hesitate not the declare, the grandest figure of ancient times, and it was from his work of regeneration, that Christ, at a later period, inspired himself, as Moses had been inspired by the works of Manes and Manu.

A few more lines and we shall have finished, too briefly, perhaps, with this redeemer, to take up the role played by his successors in India, who, step by step, forgot the sublime traditions of the Master, to plunge the people, for the benefit of their domination, into a moral degradation and abasement, that rendered possible the absorbing and despotic reign of ancient theocracies, issue, as we have seen, Indian Brahmanism.

XV

TRANSFIGURATION OF KRISHNA

Then, one day, when the tyrant of Mathura had sent a large army against Krishna and his disciples, the disciples, terrified, sought to escape by flight from the danger that menaced them.

Their faith seemed staggered; Krishna, who was praying near them, having heard their complaints, advanced to their midst, and said:—

"Why are your spirits possessed with senseless fear? Know you not, then, who is he that is with you?

"And then, abandoning the mortal form, he appeared to their eyes in all the éclat of his Divine Majesty, his brow encircled with such light that his disciples, unable to support it, threw themselves on their faces in the dust, and prayed the Lord to pardon their unworthy weakness.

And Krishna, having resumed his first form, farther said: "Have you not, faith in me? Know that, present or absent, I shall always be in your midst to protect you.

"And they, believing from what they had seen, promised never thereafter to doubt his power; and they named him Devadeveśa. (*Bhāgavata Purāṇa*)

XVI

KRISHNA AND THE TWO HOLY WOMEN, NICHDALI AND SARASVATI

Krishna walked in the neighbourhood of Mathura with his disciples, followed by a great crowd eager to behold him, and they said on all sides, "Behold him who delivered us from the tyrant who oppressed us," making allusion to Kansa, who had suffered the penalty of his crimes, and whom Krishna had killed.

And they said further, "Behold him who resuscitates the dead, heals the lame, the deaf, and the blind.

"When two women of the lowest extraction drew near to Krishna and having poured upon his head the perfumes which they had brought in a little brazen vase, they worshipped him.

And as the people murmured at their boldness, Krishna kindly said to them:

"Women, I accept your sacrifice, the little which is given by the heart is of more worth than all the riches offered by ostentation. What desire you of me?

"Lord," answered they, "the brows of our husbands are clouded with care, happiness has fled from our homes, for God has refused us the joy of being mothers.

"And Krishna having raised them, for they had knelt and were kissing his feet, said to them," Your demand shall be granted, for you have believed in me, and joy shall re-enter your houses.

"Some times thereafter, these two women named Nichadali and Saraswati were delivered each of a son, and these two children afterwards became holy personages whom the Hindus still reverence under the names of Sudāmā and Sudāśa.

XVII

KRISHNA'S DEATH

The work of redemption was accomplished, all India felt a younger blood circulate in its veins, everywhere labour, was sanctified by prayer, hope and faith wormed all hearts.

Christna (Krishna) understood that the hour had come for him to quit the earth, and to return to the bosom of him who had sent him.

Forbidding his disciples to follow him, he went, one day, to make his ablutions on the seashore and wash out the stains that his mortal envelope might have contracted in the struggles of every nature which he had been obliged to sustain against the partisans of the past.

Arrived at the seashore, he plunged himself three times therein, then, kneeling and looking to heaven, he prayed, expecting death.

In this position he was pierced with arrows by one of those whose crimes he had unveiled and who, hearing of his journey to the sea, had, with a strong troop, followed with the design of assassinating him.

This man was named Aṅgada. According to popular belief, condemned, for his crime, to an eternal life on earth, he wanders on the earth, having no other food than the remains of the dead, on which he feeds constantly, in company with jackals and other unclean animals.

The body of the God-man was suspended to the branches of a tree by his murderer, that it might become the prey of vulture.

News of the death having spread, the people came in a

crowd conducted by Arjuna, the dearest of the disciples of Krishna, to recover his sacred remains. But the mortal frame of the Redeemer had disappeared — no doubt it had regained the celestial abodes . . . and the tree to which it had been attached had become suddenly covered with great red flowers and diffused around it the sweetest perfumes.

Thus ended Krishna, victim of the wickedness of those who would not recognise his law and who had been expelled from amidst the people because of their vices and their hypocrisy. (*Bhāgavata Purāṇa* and Brahmanical traditions.)

XVIII

SOME WORDS OF EXPLANATION

I do not fear that any thinking Orientalist will come forward in the least to contradict what I have advanced about the Devakī and her son Krishna. Doubtless they have long understood that the modern myths of the Indian tradition and of poetry are the produce of decay and of the superstitions which the Brāhmaṇas allowed to impress themselves on the spirits of the masses, to profit of their own domination. If therefore, I have rejected all the heroic adventures in which Indian poets introduce Krishna it is that they are the after-inventions of the Oriental imagination, which knows no bounds in the domain of the marvellous.

The most celebrated poems on Krishna date no father back than the *Mahābhārata*, which was written more than three thousand years before our era. These productions had their origin in the idea that the Divinity is constantly occupied in directing human contents and human affairs at his will, and in distributing, even on earth, rewards and punishments to the good or to the evil-doer.

It is the same idea that pervades ancient Egyptian, Greek, and Hebrew civilisations, offspring as we have demonstrated of that period during which India, forgetting the pure traditions of the Vedas and of Krishna, threw herself into the arms of saints, of heroes, and of demi-gods.

Permit us to take an example from our modern times in exemplification of the absolute necessity of utterly repudiating Indian poetry when seeking to appreciate Krishna and of adhering to work of pure theology, to the teaching of Śāstras and to the traditions preserved in India.

Some attempts were made amongst ourselves during the sixteenth century, to supersede the introduction in epic poetry, of Mars, of Jupiter, of Juno, of Venus of Minerva, by substituting Krishna, the apostles, angels, saints. The Jerusalem delivered of Tasso had served as a model.

Had such a custom become general (and without doubt it would have succeeded in the East), would not inquire, seeking after two or three thousand years, to exhume the past, have been obliged, especially if Western civilisations had become extinct or transformed, or if Christianity had disappeared, to abjure poetry and legend, in forming a serious idea of Christ, of his Apostles and his doctrine, under pain of finding these personages mixed up in all our civil and religious wars, and being thus forced to reject them as the inventions of superstition.

My mode of procedure has been no other than this, and I have studied Krishna only by his philosophic and moral revolution; the sole point of view, moreover, under which he is considered by learned scholars, who even to-day in India consecrate their lives to the study of the law and of religious truths.

XIX

SUCCESSORS OF KRISHNA — GRANDEUR AND DECAY OF BRAHMANISM

The immediate successors of Krishna sanctified themselves by the practice of all virtues, a complete abnegation of self, and hoping only in a future life, they lived poor, and wholly occupied themselves with the celestial mission the Master had bequeathed them.

How splendid the figure of those Brahmin priests of the ancient times of India! How pure and majestic their worship, and how worthy of the God whom they served!

We shall see, according to the *Mānava-Dharma-Śāstra* and Brahmanical theology, how the priest, faithful to his duties, may with immortality; what are the moral principles he should follow; what his imperative rules of conduct; what, in a word, was the priest of primitive times, whom, it will not be uninteresting afterwards to contrast with the actual Brāhmaṇa.

Interrogating our motives of action, Manu replies self-love as little commendable, and yet he finds nothing in this world exempt from it.

"Of the hope of a possible good," says he, "is begotten the faculty of exertion: the greatest sacrifices have for object, something to acquire; devout austerities and all good actions spring from the hope of reward.

" But he immediately adds:

"He who has fulfilled all his duties to please God alone, and without expecting future recompense, is sure of immortal happiness."

"The most important of all duties is first to study the Vedas, which is the word of Brahmā and of Krishna revealed to men."

"The authority of the divine revelation (*śruti*) should be incontestable. The Brāhmaṇa priest, who would attain perfect felicity in the other world, can only do so by submitting himself, without seeking to understand or to comment upon the orders of the Lord, in what may appear to him inexplicable.

"He must also bend to tradition (*smṛti*) where law has not spoken. Thus, if it is permitted to common men to be guided by self-love, and the hope of reward, the actions of the priest should have no motive but God alone, and he has for guide through life the word of the Lord which has revealed to him his will; and tradition where Holy Scripture is silent.

"Denouncing the free-thinkers who already in his time attempted the reforms afterward realised by Buddha, who was the Luther of India, Manu hurls at them this anathema:

"Let all those who, embracing the profane opinions of the enemies of the law of God, refuse to recognise the authority of revelation and of tradition, be expelled as atheists and blasphemers of the holy books.

"The initiated Brāhmaṇa should take vow of chastity, he may not present himself at the holy sacrifice, which he must offer each morning to God, but with heart and body pure, And in prostrating himself with respect at the foot of the altar, should he read the Holy Scriptures.

The first part of his life, until about seventy years should be mendicant. He should instruct his fellows and direct them towards God, during this time he does not belong to himself; all who are unhappy, all who are afflicted, should be consoled by him. All that is little, poor, or helpless, should be sustained by him.

Let us consider him from his birth, for we may almost say that from that moment his duties begin.

The advent of Krishna upon earth, although it atoned original transgression, did not efface all stain; hence, should each one born to the faith, be purified and regenerated at birth by the sacred water of the Yamuna, or, in its default by the water of purification, or holy water consecrated by the priest's prayers in the temple.

For the Brāhmaṇa destined to become a Guru, i.e., a priest of the divine law, this ceremony of purification in not sufficient; for him is further ordained investiture with the sacred thread, and the tonsure persistently practised for life, from the age of three years.

Further, at the moment of dipping a Brāhmaṇa, his lips are to be smeared with clarified butter and honey, and during recital of the prayer of consecration.

The ceremonies and scarifies attending tonsure are to be repeated in sixth year after birth.

At sixteen years of age all men devoted to the Lord are obliged to present themselves at the temple to confirm their purification by anointment with holy oil, for at that age they enter on their majority.

After that term, saith Manu, all those who have not duly received this sacrament, are pronounced unworthy of initiation and excommunicated.

(It is impossible to translate the Sanskrit expression *Vrātyas,* otherwise than by the word excommunication, which we have employed).

When the Brāhmaṇa child understands the act, he should perform his prayers, night and morning, erect, and with joined hands; by the prayer of morning he atones the trifling faults which he may unconsciously have committed in the night; by the prayer of night he effaces the stains unconsciously contracted through the day; it is only later, and after the age of sixteen, that he can be admitted, according to the rules prescribed by the Holy Scripture, to offer sacrifice to the Divinity.

But before becoming a priest and instructor of the faithful, the Brāhmaṇa is obliged to pass many years in the schools of theology and of philosophy, where he learns the science of life, and that of God in which he should instruct others — this is the period of his noviciate.

The following are the studies he pursues:

The Sanskrit, that sacred language which God spoke when he revealed himself to men.

Theology, with a complete treatise on religious ceremonies.

Philosophy, more especially in its bearing upon what constitutes duty.

Astronomy

Mathematics

General grammar and prosody

And lastly, what is considered most essential to the priest,

The Vedas, or Holy Scriptures, with commentaries and explanations of difficult or obscure passages.

And, says Manu, if a son should love and respect his father and mother because he has received from them material life, how much more ought he to respect his instructor, his spiritual father, who has given him the life of the soul?

His noviciate over, the Brāhmaṇa becomes a consecrated servant amongst the servants of God, that is, a priest, under the following rules of conducts:-

He should subsist upon alms, that is, upon offerings made by the faithful to the temple, for he should have no possessions; should practice fasting and abstinence, show the people an example of all the virtues, and divide his time between prayer and the instruction which in his turn he should extend to neophytes.

When the Brāhmaṇa, from catechumen, has thus become priest, and then professor, when he has strewed his way with good works, and devoted the greater part of his life to the service of God and his neighbour, there remains from him a last ordeal before attaining his final absorption in the bosom of Divinity.

Let us listen to the Holy Scripture that prescribes his conduct:

"Let him be alone, without companions, and without dreaming that he is abandoned of all the world, and that he has abandoned all.

"Let him have neither hearth nor house; if hunger torment him, let him leave to God the care of his nourishment — at his feet grow the herbs he shall eat.

"Let him desire not life, nor long for death; and as a reaper at night waits peaceably for his wages at the door of the master, so let him wait until his hour is come.

"Let him purify all his actions, in consecrating them to the Lord.

"He should bear offensive words with patience, have contempt for none, and above all guard against hatred of any on behalf of this weak and perishable body.

"If he who shall strike him let fall the staff employed, let him pick it up and restore it without murmur.

(Is not this buffet of the New Testament?)

"He should never seek a subsistence by explaining prodigies and dreams.

"Let him above all guard against perverting the true spirit of the Holy scripture to educe there form precepts of a casuist morality in favour of worldly passions and interests.

(What say you, Messieurs de Loyala? This lesson comes from afar.)

"And when the hour of death shall sound for him, let him request to be extended on a mat and covered with ashes, and let his last word be a prayer for entire humanity that must continue to suffer when he is himself re-united to the Father of all things.

"Such were the priests of Brahmā of other times' their life's occupation: first, prayer and instruction; secondly, meditation on eternal truths, the Holy Scripture and the grandeur of the Supreme Being.

Priests at first, afterwards recluses, this world for them but a place of exile and expiation which should conduct them to eternal bliss in another life.

A man who passed thirty years of his life in India, and who assuredly will not be taxed with partiality in such matters, could not refrain thanks to a profound spirit of justice, from pronouncing the same judgement as ourselves upon the ancient scholars.

Here is what the missionary Dubois says of them in the second volume of his work entitled *Mœurs des Indes:*

"Justice,   humanity,   good   faith,   compassion, disinterestedness, all the virtues in fact were familiar to them, and taught to others both by precept and example. Hence it comes that the Indians profess, at least speculatively, nearly the same moral principles as ourselves; and if they do not practice all the reciprocal duties of men towards each other in a civilised society, it is not because they do not know them.

"This is what a priest of Christ did not fear to say of the priests of Krishna. Yet he was not acquainted with the numerous works on theology, philosophy and morals, which early ages have bequeathed us, and which the study of Sanskrit is now enabling us to explore.

His principles, his religious faith, would doubtless have prevented his going further in his appreciation; but what would he have said if it had been permitted him to find all his beliefs, all the ceremonies of his own worship in the primitive Indian Church?

After many ages of simplicity, abnegation and faith, the

germs of domination began to ferment in the bosom of Vedic scholars. Their ascendant once secured over the people, priests perceived the possibility of acquiring complete dominion, both civil and religious, temporal as well as spiritual, and they set about the work of bending political power to paramount religious authority.

In the first part of this work we have seen how they succeeded, by caste-divisions and by gradually allowing the people to sink into brutish abasement and the most shameless demoralisation.

We have equally seen how after ages of unresisted domination, they were powerless to resist the invading conquerors of their country, powerless to re-animate against the stranger a people whom they had long deprived of all initiative, all liberty, and consequently of al courage.

Sad example of the lot that attends peoples who identify the religious idea with the priest, submitting to his dominations to the extent of having neither freedom of judgement, freedom of conscience, nor self-respect.

In all religion that resists tolerance and freedom of judgement, the priest is but an industrious combatant against progress and liberty.

The Indians were demoralised by the priests, but the moral degradation extended even to them, and the arms they employed were turned against themselves.

The Brāhmaṇa priests of the present day are but the shadow of themselves, crushed, in their poverty, their weakness, their vices, and their actual decrepitude under memories of the past, with some very rare exception they but divide amongst them an inheritance of immense pride, which harmonises but sadly with their degradation and their inutility.

These people have no longer either dignity or self-respect, and long ago would this Brāhmaṇa caste have disappeared under public contempt, had not India been India, that is, the country, par excellence, of immobility.

If their power over the masses is still great, intelligent people of the higher castes, without avowing it, however, consider them no longer in any other light than as vagabonds, whom they are obliged by prejudice to protect and support.

Ramble of an evening through towns and country, approach wherever you hear the sound of trumpet and tom-tom, it is a birth, a marriage, or the puberty of a young girl that is being celebrated. Look under the veranda and on the stairs of the house, those ragged beggars who squall and distort themselves, those are Brāhmaṇas who come to eat the rice that has been prepared in honour of the ceremony.

This tribute is their due, and they levy it upon all classes of society, not a family festival, nor public fete can take place without it, and it is customary for them to carry off the dishes in which they have been served.

Generally these dishes are of vulgar metal, iron or brass, it sometimes, however, happens that a Rājā, impelled by pride and ostentation has the Brāhmaṇas served on dishes of silver, or of gold, and expends a million for that purpose, the Brāhmaṇas are then satisfied and exhaust all Oriental hyperbole in the praises they address to the liberal prince; but it is rare that they are not obliged afterwards to separate them, the division of their riches requiring some interchange of blows from the ratan.

There are, however, a few members of this debased caste who have rigidly separated themselves from it. Some have consoled themselves for the loss of power by plenary return to the primitive faith, and it is not rare to find in southern India, Brāhmaṇa priests living midst study and prayer, and presenting to the people, who reverence them as saints, the most perfect example of all virtues, Others, taking a more forward stride, renouncing parents, friends, and rebelling against present miseries, have devoted themselves to preaching the equality of all men, and the regeneration of their country by opposition to the stranger.

From contact with Europeans they have discovered that

their weakness and inferiority resulted wholly from their stagnant inertia and their divisions of caste; and, anxious to shake off the yoke, they endeavour to revivify the enervated blood that flows in the veins of their compatriots, and to unite them against the common enemy.

Impotent efforts — which may perhaps bear fruit in the future; for the present they have but resulted in placing their authors under the national index, expelled from the bosom of their families and repudiated even by their own children.

Side by the side with the Brāhmaṇa is gradually arising an other caste which already covers a portion of southern India, with perceptible, although carefully disguised pretensions, some day to supersede them in their popular domination: they are the Community caste, composed of a multitude of fanatics who dream of the reconstruction of Brahmanism in their country, for their own profit; they begin to exercise a real influence.

Living only upon rice and vegetables, and imposing upon the people by the austerity of their manners, the members of this caste will soon command a force of immense weight in all countries — that of wealth.

The entire commerce is in their hands; they support each other by vast associations, accumulate capital, centralise, traffic, and very certainly would become a formidable, power, but for the English who fleece them under pretext of imposts; for their object is the complete restoration of that past theocracy so dear to India.

Such is the semi-brutified condition into which priests have plunged this unhappy country, that the entire population would, if left to itself, contribute its whole force to any movement that would replace it under Brahmanical authority — but for that, it must not be ruled by England's iron hand, nor for more than a century has cast envious glance over the Himalayas, on the rich plains of India— waiting the hour to seize them.

I will dwell no more in this chapter on the state of profound demoralisation into which the sacerdotal caste, abusing the religious idea, have involved India; I shall have occasion to fathom this subject more deeply in treating of the feasts and ceremonies which have supplanted those of the ancient worship.

XX

CEREMONIES AND SACRAMENTS (*SANSKĀRAS*) OF ANCIENT BRAHMANICAL WORSHIP

In ancient, as in modern religions, worship assumed two forms:

By the first, under the name of ceremonies and *yajñas*, it addressed to the Divinity the prayers and vows of mortals.

By the second, under the name of sacraments, it impose upon the faithful certain acts, certain expiations or purification; it regulates, in a word, their spiritual life, their relations with God.

We are about to see what are the *Yajña*s and the sacraments instituted by the successors of Krishna in the later Brahmanical Church.

Sarvamedha Yajña

Brāhmaṇa is considered by the Vedas as having sacrificed him for creation. Not only did God incarnate Himself aspire, to regenerate and lead us back to us divine source, but. He even immolated Himself to give us existence. "Sublime idea, which we find expressed," says M. De Humboldt, "in all the sacred books of antiquity."

Hence, say the holy books:

"Brāhmaṇa is at once performer of *yajña* and material of oblation for *yajña*, so that the priest who officiates every mornings at the ceremonies of *Sarvamedha* (universal sacrifice, symbolic of creation), in presenting his offering to God, identifies himself with the divine who is Brāhmaṇa; or rather it is Brāhmaṇa manifested in the form of Krishna, come to die upon earth for our salvation, who himself accomplishes the solemn sacrifice."

Thus the priest at the altar, in the sacrifice of *Sarvamedha* presents his offerings and his prayers to God in honour of creation and of the incarnation of Krishna.

We shall presently find the Catholic idea applying the same symbolic meaning to the sacrifice of the Mass.

This ceremony is the most important of all in Brahmanical religion; the priest cannot proceed each morning until after full examination of his faults, and purification after the prescribed manner.

The others are but secondary *yajñas*, sometimes in honour of holy personages who have attained the abodes of the blessed; sometimes to call down God's blessing upon harvests and fruits.

The materials of *yajña*s are; consecrated oil, purified water, incense, and a certain number of other perfumes, which are burnt at the altar on a tripod of gold. The offering consists of a cake of rice moistened with clarified butter, which the priest should eat after having offered it to God and sanctified it by his prayers.

Later, when Brahmanism reserved its pure doctrines and simple ceremonies for the initiated and adepts, and after the division of the people into castes, vulgar worship adopted the sacrifices of animals, which, after consecration, were divided amongst the assistants, who by this food were purified of light and involuntary faults.

It is this second epoch that inspired Egypt and the worship of Moses.

We have dwelt sufficiently on all these things, and shall not recur to them.

Sacraments (*Sanskāras*)

Within three days after birth the child should be sprinkled, that is purified by the sacred water of the Ganges or, if too distant, by the water of purification which has been consecrated by Brāhmaṇas in the pagoda.

This religious custom is very ancient in India; it dates from the Vedic epoch, and Krishna himself consecrated it by going before his death to plunge into the water of the Ganges; it is still in honour amongst Indian, who fail not to observe it with all ceremonies of the ancient rite.

The sacred books of India loudly assert that the object in sprinkling of the infant, is to wash away the stain of oriental transgression.

However, it be, and if we consider this as a simple ablution — the form is imposed by religion, and is accomplished by a Brāhmaṇa which suffices to place it amongst the sacraments.

Moreover, this religious custom is not isolated, the water of purification, which has purified the infant, continues to purify him whenever used during the course of his existence; hence, doubles, the system of ablutions adopted by all Oriental religions.

Of Confirmation.

Let us, without comment, confine ourselves on this subject to citation of two texts: one from the Vedas and the other from Manu.

Athrva Veda.

"Whoever shall not, before the age of sixteen, have had his purification confirmed in the temple by unction of holy oil, by consecrated investiture, and the prayer of the Sāvitrī, should be expelled from the midst of the people as despiser of the divine word."

Notwithstanding division of the people into castes, and perversion of ancient doctrines, the Brāhmaṇas preserved this sacrament, and extended it to all classes, except the Śudras, or proletariats, slaves, and parias.

Manu, abridged and modified to suit their interest, speaks thus (book ii. *śloka* 38 & 39):

Until the 12th year of a Brāhmaṇa until the 16 for a   Kṣ

atriya until the 18 for *Vaiśya*, and 20 for a *Śudra*, the time for receiving investiture sanctified by the *Sāvitrī*, is not yet passed.

"But beyond these terms, the young men of these three classes, who have not duly received this sacrament, shall be declared unworthy of initiation, excommunicated (*Vrâtyas*) and delivered over to the contempt of honest men."

In collating these two texts we perceive that his sacrament of confirmation was a continuation of the first ceremony performed at the infant's cradle, that is, a confirmation of the purification by water within three days after birth.

Purification and Absolution. Confession.

According to Indian tradition, man is subject on earth to different taints — some of the soul, others of the body.

Contaminations of the body are effaced sometimes by simple water, at others by the water of purification, according to their gravity, sometimes by abstinence and mortification.

And on this subject we may say that it is difficult to form an idea of the tortures and flagellations which hermits imposed, and which the Fakirs, their successors still impose upon themselves in India.

Impurities of the soul are effaced by prayer, by penances, and pilgrimages to the Ganges, as well as to different places sanctified by the life and the death of Krishna.

As may be easily conceived, under the empire of this absorbing religion which at last so governed both soul and body of its adepts as to regulate the most insignificant usages of daily life, man was no more allowed to judge his own faults, than he was permitted to question Holy Scripture.

For, as says Manu, book first:

"The birth of the priest is the eternal incarnation of justice; the priest is born to administer justice, for in his judgements he identifies himself with God."

"The priest in coming into the world, is placed in the highest rank of earth; sovereign lord of all beings, it is for him to watch over conservation of the treasures of civil and religious laws."

As religious judge the priest knew all sins, and all transgressions, and indicated the expiations to be performed by the guilty— in this manner:

Each morning, after *yajña*, those who felt themselves reprehensible, assembled in the court of the pagoda near the sacred tank, and there, at a table presided over by the oldest of the priests, they confessed their faults, and received the sentence imposed upon them.

The formula of confession was as follows:

"The Brāhmaṇa guardians of the Divine Śruti (revelations), you who know the expiating *sanskāras* (sacraments), what ought to do?" Stating faults.

And the senior Brāhmaṇa would answer:

"Enlightened by the Divine Spirit, we have decided, and this is what you ought to do. . . ."

And then, according to the gravity of the offence, the religious tribunal imposed either ablutions, mortifications, and abstinence, fines or offerings to God, prayers or pilgrimages."

The offences which no purification could atone (see the enumeration, Chap. V of Part First) were punished by partial or complete privation of caste. The excommunicated (*Vrâtyas*) alone fell to the rank of parias.

To explain the expression "*sanskāras*" of the formula above cited, and which we have translated *sacrament,* we cannot do better then quote the following annotations of the Orientalist Loiseleur Deslonchamps, the translator of Manu.

"The sacraments (*sanskāras*) are purificatory ceremonies intended for the civilisation process of an individual Marriage is the last sacrament."

We were therefore justified in calling the absolution of the Indian, by the Brāhmaṇa priest, a sacrament, following public confession.

We shall presently find early Christians adopting this custom, thanks, no doubt, to the many traditions, of India studied by their first instructions in Egypt and the East.

Marriage was also held as a sacrament by the Vedic religion; it is so established by the following text of the Vedas;

"Brahmā created marriage in creating the man and the woman for reproduction of the human species; also, in memory of the divine work, the union of the sexes, to be valid, should be consecrated by prayers of the priest."

According to the note of Loiseleur Deslonchmaps, above cited, and which we recognise as correct, Death is the last of the sacraments, for it is remarkable that the Indian priest did not directly intervene at the pillow of the dying. The Vedic religion in such circumstances conferred the right to officiate on the eldest son or nearest relation of the sick, who was charged to accomplish the funeral ceremonies in fulfilment of this text of scripture.

"At the hour of death it is the prayer of the son that opens to the father the abode of the blessed."

Briefly, the Vedic sacraments are five in number:

Ist. The anointing the priest, consecrated servant amongst all the servants of God. We have seen, in studying the education required of a human being.

2nd. Ablution or baptism of the newly-born in the waters of the Ganges, or in the waters of purification.

3rd. Confirmation, at the age of 12 for Brāhmaṇas, 16 Kṣ atriyas, and twenty for *Vaiśyas*, and twenty four for *Śudras*. of the purification at the cradle of the newly-born.

4th. Absolution of faults, by public confession.

5th Marriage.

We have said little about this last sacrament, and the reason is plain.

There can be no discussion on this point, for it is a vulgar truth needing no demonstration, that ancient societies have all considered marriage as a religious tie.

XXI

BRAHMANICAL FEASTS AND CEREMONIES OF THE PRESENT TIME

The mass of Hindus of the present day have but a feeble impression of their ancient worship, and the Brāhmaṇas, after having despotically perverted the loftiest and purest Principles have in their turn sunk into the moral degradation which they fostered for the maintenance of their own authority. When invasions had ruined their political power, they took refuge in their temples, multiplied feasts and ceremonies, and emulated each other in pomp and splendour to preserve their religious prestige.

It may not be without interest to see, from description of a Hindu fete, to what degree of habitude the priests had reduced the people, after having proscribed during their domination, all civil and religious liberties; and that, too, in the name of God, who has always been in Europe, as in Asia, the grand pretence of all sacerdotal castes.

Let those same liberties be proscribed amongst ourselves, and if we do not sink to Oriental degradation, we shall, without doubt, retrograde to the subjection of the middle ages, to the religious thraldom of kings and people, to Torquemada, the grand inquisitor and his executioners, inflicting torture with crucifix in hand.

It would be quite impossible for me to give even the simplest nominal list of the fetes of Indian worship, which, however, are all alike, with more or less pomp and solemnity, according to the richness of the temple where they are celebrated, and the amount of offerings of the faithful.

Saints and heroes have been so multiplied that the three hundred and sixty-five days of the year are insufficient to honour them all, even if passed in batches, as many as possible each day.

Brahmanism has almost completely lost the idea of God, and has replaced his worship by that of Devas or angles, and Ṛṣis or saints; and such infallibly must be the end of all religion that refuses to submit itself to the light of reason.

We will take as example one of the feasts, that of Chidambrum of southern India, which, in the midst of existing superstitions, has still preserved an appearance of grandeur.

This feast commences five days before the new moon of May, and ends five days after, without a minute's intermission, without affording a moment's repose to the immense crowd of pilgrims and devotees assembled to assist from all parts of India.

The first eight days are passed in the interior of the temple, Hindus of high caste being alone admitted, the common people remain in the courts, content from far to hear the music and the sacred chants.

The first day is consecrated to Śiva, and solely employed to celebrate his beneficent action on nature; it is by him that from decomposition springs to germs that produces the rice, so useful to man, the perfumed flowers, and the lofty trees that adorn the earth with their foliage.

During night they chant the mysterious union of God with Nature, and salute the rising sun by a hymn to the holy personage Kārtikeya, whose prayers relieved the earth from the demon Kayamongāsura, who had come to torment humanity, under the form of a monster with the head of an elephant.

The second day is devoted to prayer for the souls of ancestors. At night they are offered (consecrated) boiled rice, honey, clarified butter, and fruits. Once devoted to the manes, these aliments have the property of effacing all impurities.

They are distributed to the assistants, who, having eaten them, should immediately go and plunge into the sacred tank which is found on one side of the temple.

The third day passes in supplications to the Poulêars, protecting divinities of villages and farms, a sort of peanuts; at night are blessed the images of these gods, brought by the faithful, who afterwards place them in their houses, or on the borders of their fields to protect their limits.

The fourth and following night are assigned to celebration of the river Kaveri, whose water have the same purifying properties as those of the Ganges, for those who, from poverty or infirmity, are unable, at least once in their lives, to make the pilgrimage to the great river.

The fifth is the day of offerings— the fervent press in crowds under the portals bringing rice, oil, and the sandal-woods of which is made the odorous powder that burns in tripods of gold and vases of price.

Brāhmaṇas excel in the art of exciting the emulation of rich Hindu to rivalry in the magnificence of their presents.

On the sixth day they pray that the enterprises of those who have especially distinguished themselves by their gifts, may not be obstructed by any evil genius — and the day following, at the first hour of the day, a Brāhmaṇa announces what days of the year will be lucky and unlucky.

The seventh day, especially devoted to women who have not yet conceived, is employed in supplications to Śiva to accord them a happy fecundity; such as more especially desire an end to their sterility, should pass the night in the pagoda, under the protection of *God!*

The Brāhmaṇas avail themselves of the obscurity and of the agitation excited in them by the place, to prostitute them amongst themselves, and give themselves up to a night of orgic and debauch. They then persuade these poor creatures, timid and credulous to excess, that they have been visited by superior spirits sent to them by Śiva himself.

Nor is it rare for women of the highest caste, and of

exquisite beauty, to be thus delivered to strangers, who pay very large sums to the priest to be secretly introduced into the pagoda during this nights.

The eighth day is wholly occupied in dressing the monstrous car, which the next day is to make the tour of the pagoda, bearing the colossal statue of the god Śiva; drawn by his worshippers.

The ninth day, at eleven of the morning to the sound of guns, fireworks and chants of music, two thousand Hindu burst through the crowd to attach themselves to the car of the god, high as a monument and covered with allegoric sculptures.

All at once an immense acclamation bursts upon the air the bayadêres keep time as they force back the crowds, the priest intone the sacred hymn, thousands of censers fill the air with the smoke of their incense. It is the car that begins its triumphal march, one, two, three acclamations are heard, the crowed applauding shouts :— It is at some fakirs who come to throw themselves to be crushed under the car of the god. The blood gushes under the wheels, and, at the risk of the same fate, devotees rush to dip in the human liquor a piece of cloth which they will preserve as a precious relic.

When the sacred car has made its course round the temple, the ceremony is over for that day, and some repose is necessary to prepare for the grand fête of the night of the following day.

This is the moment for the stranger to enter the courts and dependences of the temple to visit the fakirs and Saṁnyāsis.

The Saṁnyāsis are mendicant pilgrims, who have accomplished the pilgrimage to the Ganges, in fulfilment of vows, each more extraordinary than the other.

Some have gone to the banks of the sacred river in measuring the distance with their bodies.

Others have made the same march on their hands and knees.

Others, again, in tying their feet together and jumping the whole distance, or in restricting themselves to eating and sleeping only every three days during the journey.

It is well to know that it is nearly six hundred leagues from Chidambrum to the nearest branch of the river Kaveri.

But this is nothing, and the folly of all these people is greatly surpassed by the fanaticism of fakirs, who sit impassable and smiling in the midst of suffering the most hideous, of tortures the most frightful.

Look at that wheel turns with such rapidity, carrying with it five or six human figures who redden the earth with their blood; these are fakirs who have suspended themselves with iron hooks passed through their thighs, their loins, or their shoulders.

Near them we remark another seated on a plank studded with long points of iron which deeply penetrate his flesh.

See that man who, with the aid of a tube, sucks in a little broth from a plate,— he has condemned himself to silence, and to make it impossible for him to break his vow, he has burnt his lips with a red hot-iron and stitched them together to become united, leaving in the middle a small hole that can only admit fluid aliment.

His neighbour is obliged to eat like an animal, out of dish, unable for many years past to make use of his hands, having so bound them together with cocoa-cords that the points of the right hand nails press on the palm of the left, and vice-versa. The nails have grown and united the two hands to each other, penetrating the flesh and muscles through and through.

What horrible mutilations! a few steps and we are sickened at the sight. But let us on, there is still more frightful infliction, and not a complaint, not a cry; one would say that these men have conquered pain.

What is that inert mass stretched upon the earth which we should suppose inanimate, did it not appear occasionally to breathe? Its arms, its legs are twisted and ankayrosed, it has neither nose nor ears, its lips excised to the very edge of the gums, lay bare the opening teeth— horror! This canvas has no longer a tongue, it looks like a death's-head. It is really a man?

Near is a woman who has no longer the indication of sex, she has burnt or cut them away. Her body is but one vast ulcer — half rotten — the worms feed upon it.

Another is stretched upon a bed of burning charcoal, he will extinguish it with his flesh and his blood.

Neat the tank which serves to wash the statues of gods and saints, and for holy ablutions, a fakir groans under a pile of wood that weighs at least two or three hundred kilograms, while another buried in earth to the very neck receives the sun's ray sin al their scorching heat upon his skull, shaven to the very skin.

Let us stop; the sight becomes wearied, as the pen refuses longer to describe such scenes.

Who, then, can urge men to impose such tortures upon themselves? What fanatic and senseless faith if they really think thus to make themselves agreeable to God! What courage and what stoicism if it is but jugglery!

It is said that the Brāhmaṇas, whose purpose they serve in astonishing and stupefying the crowd, bring them up for their role from the tenderest age, and that they bestialize the body and fanaticise the spirit of these unfortunates by seclusion, and the promise of immortal recompense.

During the night of the tenth day, which is the last of the fête, the statue of Śiva is promenaded on this tank of the pagoda, of which it should make the tour seven times.

I could not describe in all its details the bizarre and grandiose eccentricity of this scene, which suddenly bursts forth as by enchantment, in the midst of Bengal fireworks of all colours, launched from a hundred thousand hands.

The atmosphere is obscured by smoke from golden tripods

where constantly burn perfumed balls that turn upon themselves, tracing in the night a circle of fire; the dazzled crowds become frantic on the steps—stamp—shout in honour of the god. At moments the Bengal fire ceasing, the obscurity for some seconds is almost complete, the enormous statue of the idol alone, splendidly illuminated, silently over the waters-at its feet recline the bayadêres in the most enchanting attitudes, then blaze forth most gorgeous fires, with accompanying frantic hurrahs.

The seventh tour is nearly completed, the chants become shrieks, the delirium reaches its climax; men, women, and children plunge into the tank to purify themselves in the water that Śiva has just traversed.

Woe to the paria who had dared to enter the gates of the temple: if recognised at such a moment, he would be infallibly torn in pieces.

Such is the exaltion, that even if it pleased the officiating Brāhmaṇa, in the name of God, to denounce the Europeans who assist a the ceremony, to the anger of the crowd, not one of them would escape alive from the enclosure.

About four in the morning Śiva is reconducted with great pomp into the mysterious interior of the pagoda, not to be again exhibited until the next year; the fires slowly die out, the crowd gradually disperses to the sound of sacred trumps and tum-tums, the stranger retires, unable at first to account to him-self for the different emotions that have assailed him.

The most magnificent fêtes of the North of India—that is, of Bengal— are miserable compared with those of the South.

In the south, where Mohammedan invasion was less firmly established where the sectarian intolerance of Omar and of Hyder Ali has not razed temples and bend consciences to the law of the sword and the crescent, it would appear that Brahmanical domination has presented something of its ancient prestige.

There have religious traditions found refuge in the hearts

of some few learned Brāhmaṇas, who preserve the precious deposit in the hope of an approaching regeneration.

There are the grand monuments, the gigantic ruins, the majestic God, sculptured in granite of fifty feet high, there, in fact, are the remains of that old Vedic civilisation that inspired the entire of Asia, Greece, Egypt, Judea, and Rome.

It is there, we cannot repeat it too often, there is our field of study and of research.

The few savants who have visited India have invariably thrown themselves upon Calcutta and Bengal, where the Indians, from European contact, has opened shops, and becomes a dealer in rice and indigo.

They have not perceived that the North of India has lost its stamp, that Mohammedan temples have replaced pagodas, and English cottages the palaces of Rājas and that they were but visiting the field of battle of all the invasions that have decimated India, to which have succeeded the European agiotage. (This is the evidence of Hindu temples converting into Mosques and the palaces into the English colleges. Editor)

The festivals of Bengal do not assemble those imposing masses that are seen on the Eastern point of India, the Karnatic or the Malayala, for instance.

Each family has its own fete and after its own manner, and unity has much to do with this separation.

The high castes will have no contact with the inferior castes, nor the rich with the poor. It is necessary that people should say, while gazing at the procession of a statue ornamented with gold and jewels, and followed by people in silks and cashmeres, "That is the Puja of Babu such a one." If we make a display, the world must be informed who pays for it.

It is in some degree European pride grafted upon that of the Indian. Many members of the high castes even disdain to show themselves in public processions, and pay substitutes to follow the idol in their name.

The only festival of Bengal, which has some splendour and a certain affluence of devotees, is the Puja of September, festival of Brahmā and of Nature, but it is distinguished by nothing truly original; it is but a tissue of gross and often disgusting buffoonery.

It must be confessed that the Bengalese have a singular way of honouring God; they exhibit for the occasion, without respect for women or children, images the most obscene and disgusting and on their stages represent scenes of indecency that pass at bounds. Thus I once saw this fete celebrated at Hoogly, a small village on the Ganges, after the following manner: a man and a woman, the one representing Brahmā, the other Nature, on a public scaffolding, deliberity consummate the act of generation, as I was assured, in honour of the germs fecundated by God at Creation.

What can be expected from a people sunk into such social brutisness? And let it be well understood that it has been produced by abuse of the religious idea and by priestly domination.

Never could the reign of reason have conduced to such orgies — to such as oblivion of sane doctrines and of self-respect.

And let us not feel assured that our enlightened European civilisations could never engender similar decrepitude. Let the same causes be permitted to operate, and we shall see the same results.

Let us not forget the mysteries performed in our middle ages by the brothers of the Passion, and the *clercs of the basoche* (a short of ecclesiastical court) even in the sanctuaries of the temples, and which at last proscribed because of their obscenities, and, sad to say, these proscription emanated from royal ordinances, and not from religious censures.

If free judgement had not succeeded in establishing itself;

if we had continued to torture and to burn for a Bible-text; if kings, as in India, had accepted tutelage without murmur and without resistance, — where should we have been? Answer, where should we be?

We have got beyond that period, it will be said, and the people who have conquered civil and religious liberty will not retrograde!

Who knows?

Had not India its epoch of free judgement, free discussion, and of liberty? The sacerdotal class strove without relaxation; patient, it pursed its work— ages did not weary it, — and it conquered.

The contest threatens again to receive between liberty and religious despotism — what do I say? It is already everywhere engaged.

The most imposing manifestation of the age is to be made in a few months at Rome against the principles of '89.

Let us watch — and prepare our defence.

XXII

LAST MANIFESTATION OF GOD ON EARTH, ACCORDING TO INDIAN SACRED BOOKS

According to Indian beliefs, the *Mahāpralaya*, the grand dissolution, that is, the end of the world, will be signalised by a strange event:-

Let Ramatsariar, the religious commentator on the sacred books, speak:-

" .... Some times before the destruction of all that exists, the struggle between *Dharma* and *Adharma* must recommence on earth, and the *Adharma* who, at their first creation, rebelled in heaven against the authority of Brahmā, will present themselves for a final struggle to dispossess God of his power and recover their liberty."

Then will Krishna again come upon earth, to overthrow the prince of the Rākṣasas, who through *Aśvamedha* will cover the globe with ruins and with carnage.

The belief is general in India, there is not an Indian whatever caste he belongs, not a Brāhmaṇa that does not consider it as an article of faith. The priests have even performed *Aśvamedha Yajña* for the future victory of the son of the Devakī.

I state and record the fact without present comment.

XXIII

A TEXT OF THE PHILOSOPHER NĀRADA

"Never resort to the argument: 'I do not know this, — therefore it is false.'

"We must study to know, know to comprehend, and comprehend to judge."

In closing these studies on the religious beliefs and sacred books of India, I say the same to all contradiction.

Before judging me, study the old civilisation of the East, and I shrink from no discussion, fear no light.

Epilogue

INUTILITY AND IMPOTENCE OF THE CHRISTIAN MISSIONARY IN INDIA

If, as has said the Rev. Father Dubios **justice, humanity, good faith, compassion, disinterestedness, in fact, all the vitues, were familiar to the Ancient Indians.**

If it is true, to maintain equally with him, that the Hindu, profess the same moral principles as we do, we have the key to our complete missionary failure in India— failure, moreover, avowed by a great number amongst them who either care not or dare not explain the reason.

"Why should I change my religion?" demanded a Brāhmaṇa, with whom I was one day discussing these matters."

" Ours is as good as yours, if not better, and you but date it all since eighteen centuries, while our belief is continuous without interruption from the creation of the world.

"God, according to you, and you thus diminish him, required several efforts to provide you with a religion — according to us, he revealed his law in creating us.

"Whenever man has strayed, He has manifested Himself, to recall him to the primitive faith.

"Lastly, he incarnated himself in the person of Krishna who came, not to instruct humanity in new laws, but to efface original sin and purify morals.

This incarnation you have adopted, as you have adopted our tradition of the creation of *Ādima* and Heva.

"We shall expect another, before the end of the world, that of Christna (Krishna) coming to encounter the Prince of the *Rākṣasas* disguised as a horse, and from what you have just told me of your Apocalypse, you have also borrowed this prophecy from us.

"Your religion is but an infiltration, a souvenir of ours, wherefore then desire me to adopt it?

"if you would succeed, do not begin by teaching me principles that I find in all our holy books, and a morale which we possess in India from long before Europe had opened its eyes to the light of civilisation."

All this was but the exact truth, and admitted no reply.

What, then, would you offer these people? A form of worship? External ceremonies? They are but visible manifestations, and not the base of a religion, and what is to be done when the bases are the same?

No doubt the Hindus have forgotten their primitive beliefs, and the purity of Christna's (Krishna's) morale, in practice, but their demoralisation is not the result of ignorance; they have perfect knowledge of their dogmas, and of all the grand principles of conscience.

Let Europe not be so ready to cast the stone; — in the midst of her strifes and her ambitions of all kinds, she would be very ill advised to give herself the palm of morality.

Doubtless the Hindu of today have substituted the most superstitious practices for worship. What else? Thanks to their priests, they have ended by deserting God, to adore the workers of miracles, angels, and saints, Devas, and Ṛṣis.

And then? Have we not also our miracles of Salette and other places, our saints, who heal the lame, the deaf, the blind —scrofula and chilblains?

Why should not the Hindu have theirs?

I happened one day to be in a village near Trichnapally, a large city on the east coast of India, where a newly arrived missionary was seeking proselytes. A Brāhamaṇa theologian presented himself, as is the practice under such circumstances, and proposed to him a public discussion on such religious matters as he might choose.

The priest, who perfectly understood the Tamil, consented; had he refused he would have sunk in the public opinion, and any Hindu, in the district to whom he might wish to speak of religion, would infallibly have answered, "Why are you afraid to measure yourself with our Brāhmaṇa?

The meeting was fixed for the following Sunday. The Indians are very fond of these encounters, of these wordy wars; men, women, and children assemble, listen with interest, become excited by the contest, and what would scarcely be believed, pursue the vanquished with pitiless hootings, and with the most perfect impartiality, be it the Brāhmaṇa or the missionary.

We shall be less surprised at this when it is known that there is not a Hindu, whatever his rank or caste, who does not know the principles of Holy Scripture, that is, of the Vedas and who does not perfectly know how to read and write.

There is a Hindu proverb which says : 'He is not a man who does not know how to fix his thought upon an olle' (a palm leaf, prepared for writing).

Sunday came, the whole village assembled under the refreshing shade of a vast Banyan, etc. etc.

PART SECOND

INDIAN ORIGIN OF JUDAISM

MOSES OR MOÏSE AND HEBREW SOCIETY

In this part we shall study the procedure of Moses which we shall explain by that of Krishna (Christna), the greatest of philosophers we venture to say, not only of India but of the entire world.

LOUIS JACOLLIOT

I

INDIAN ORIGIN OF JESUS

(ZEUS-JEZEUS-ISIS-JESUS)

Devas in Sanskrit, signifies God, supreme; it is the epithet of Brahmā -- non-operating, unrevealed, before creation. This name expresses in itself all the attributes of the Supreme Being, Brahmā Viṣṇu and Śiva.

This expression of Devas travelled to Greece with the Indian immigrants with the slight modification, and became Zeus. For Greece also it equally represented God in His pure essence-- in His mystic existence ; when He awakes from His repose and reveals Himself in action, the supreme Being receives in Greek mythology, the name of Zeuṣ pater, that is, Jupiter, God, Father, Creator, Master of Heaven and Men.

The Latin, adopting this Sanskrit word Devas makes modification; and the name of Devas becomes Deus whence the French derived the expression of Dieu, with a significant identity with Sanskrit *Deva*.

God is, in fact in the Christian idea, the name of the Symbolic Being, uniting in himself all the attributes of the three persons of the Trinity-- Father, Son, and Holy Ghost.

Assuredly I do not invent either the affinities of names, or of historic facts, either the identities of civilisations, or the similitude of language which lead me to discover in the East and in India, the cradle of our race. I desire to be logical, and never attempt to consider a fact in its isolation, to explain it by itself, or by chance, and to show that if man descends from man, the fatal corollary of this truth is to make nations emanate from other nations, more ancient.

There is here, I repeat, no new system; it is but the logic of reason applied to the logic of history.

I cannot too much insist upon this: every one admits modern imitations of the ancients, whom they suppose to have lighted the torch of primitive civilisation. Well, soon or late we must make up our mind, and admit that antiquity copied India more servilely than it has been copied by us.

We must be content to mitigate our unequalled admiration of centuries, and those men who are continually presented to us as models, who have had only imitators and knew no precursors. No doubt they gave a brilliant éclat to the primordial light they had received from the East; but that éclat should not be permitted to ignore precursor civilisations.

It is scarce a century since India became revealed to us. Very small is the number of those who have had the courage to explore, on the soil, the monuments, the manuscripts, all the boundless treasures of its first ages. Some have devoted life to the study of Sanskrit, and sought to popularise the taste in Europe.

The harvest surpassed all expectation. But what does not yet remain to be discovered, to be revealed! We have recovered the primitive language, that, perhaps, murmured by the first man; some translated fragments have come to inform us that the unity of God, the immortality of the Soul, that all our beliefs, moral and philosophic, were not merely of yesterday's growth; the obscurity of the past begins to disperse. *En avant*, then! always forward; and research will at last make the light so clear as to preclude denial.

But for that we must advance as to the conquest of the exact sciences, shut the door against dreams, idealism, and mystery, receive only as axiom, God and reason, and be persuaded that the civilisations that preceded us on earth did not die out without bequeathing to their successors the influence of their ideas and of their examples.

INDIAN ORIGIN OF BIBLE OF MOSES

At the commencement of my researches, I, one day, said to a rationalist:

"I am persuaded that Moses must have constructed his Bible from the sacred book of the Egyptians, who themselves received them from India."

"It would require proofs," was the reply.

"But," I continued, "do you not know that he was initiated by the priests at the court of Pharaoh? Is it not, then, reasonable to conclude that he utilised the knowledge he had acquired, when constructing institutions for the Hebrews?

" It would require proofs."

"Do you then consider him a messenger of God?"

"No, but proofs would not be inconvenient."

"What! does not your intelligence discover in the fact that Moses studied for more than thirty years in Egypt, ignorant even of his own Hebrew origin, a striking proof in favour of the opinion I have just expressed! Let us then obliterate this succession of ages which may obscure our judgement."

"Do you suppose that a European, called upon to construct laws and a worship for one of the savage tribes of central Africa, would think of inventing that worship and those laws, instead of employing the knowledge acquired in his own country, modified and adapted to the capacities of the people whom he desired to regenerate?"

"Such an opinion would certainly be illogical."

"Well! and then?"

"Your reasoning is sound; but believe me our old Europe loves its fetiches; if you touch Moses, give proofs, still proofs, always proofs."

And this is why, instead of simply comparing the works of Manu and the Vedas with the works of Moses:

The work of Christna (Krishna) and that of Christ:

And saying, this is derived from that. I preferred to show, in support of this opinion, that the entire western antiquity had its origin in the East and in India, in such a way as to leave to my adversaries but the alternative of denying all--which is to admit all.

Thus, as we have seen, the name, which all nations have assigned the Supreme Being, comes from the Sanskrit expressions Devas.

Devadeveśa, another Sanskrit expression, signifying the pure divine essence, was very certainly the root, the radical origin, of a crowd of other names of antiquity borne alike by gods and by distinguished men. Such as Isis, the Egyptian goddess; Josue, in Hebrew, Jousuah, the successor of Moses; Josias, king of the Hebrews; and Jeseus or Jesus; in Hebrew, Josuah.

The name of Jesus, or Jeseus, or Jeosuah, very common with the Hebrews, was in ancient India the title, the consecrated epithet assigned to all incarnations of Shri Devas or as all legislators adopted the name of Manu.

The officiating Purohita in temples and pagodas still accord this title of Devadeveśa, or pure essence, or divine emanation, only to Krishna, who is alone recognised as the word, the true incarnation, by the Vaiṣṇavites.

We simply state these etymological affinities, of which we can understand all the importance: they will hereafter become a valuable support.

Prejudiced criticism will, we doubt not, do its utmost to refute the opinion that assigns a common origin to those different names; it will not succeed in obliterating their striking resemblance; and that suffices us.

Let who will refer these resemblances to chance, that great resort of desperate argument, we shall surely have the support of all thoughtful and independent spirits.

II

INDIAN ORIGIN OF MOSES

(THE PARIAS OF EGYPT AND MOSES)

These refuse of caste, these parias of Egypt, tempted by Moses with the hope of liberty, became progenitors of the Hebrews, of that nation pompously called the people of God.

It is impossible to adopt any other conclusion as to the regeneration of this servile race, when we examine whether is their *ensemble* or their details, all the societies of that epoch.

If India has its parias Greece had its helots.

If Egypt had its outcasts, Rome had its servile class, to which she long refused the name of citizen.

It was completely in the spirit of ancient people to provide themselves with slaves, whether by conquest or by the degradation of criminals as outcasts from society, even in their descend ants; and, if we make the Hebrews descend from the outcast classes of Egypt, it is that in exploring the most remote historic traditions, it does not appear that they could have been reduced to servitude by the vicissitudes of war; and that, as a people, they but date from Moses.

However, we must choose between this origin, rational and conformable to the social state of ancient civilisation; and that which Moses himself assigns his people in two first books of the Bible,--Genesis and Exodus.

Let us see, then, what this legislator must have been. From this inquiry will result proofs as convincing as possible to give, after a lapse of near four thousand years, or an epoch which fables and legends of all kinds have contributed not a little to envelop in clouds and obscurity.

According to Moses himself, the Hebrews having

multiplied to such extent as to form a nation within a nation, and seriously to alarm Pharaoh, who then reigned, he sought by every means in his power to destroy them, notably by ordering the destruction at birth of all male infants: a poor woman unable to suffer the death of her infant before her eyes, preferred exposing him in a willow basket on the Nile.

The daughter of Pharaoh, who had come to the river-side with her attendants, to bathe, perceived the infant, and, touched with pity, saved its life, and having it conveyed to her palace, adopted it as her son.

This infant was Moses.

Brought up at the court of the kings of Egypt, even to the age of forty years, without being informed of his origin, he was one fine day, constrained to fly to the desert for killing an Egyptian who was maltreating a Hebrew, and it was there that God came to reveal to him his destined mission.

I ask, even of the most prepossessed, if it is not natural and logical to conclude, that Moses, brought up by the priests, was initiated by them in the pure worship and the learning of the higher classes, and that thence came his enlightenment?

And afterwards, when expelled from the palace of Pharaoh, whether from exposure of his origin, which had been concealed by the princess who saved him, or, as he himself tells us, for having killed an Egyptian, would not resentment and the desire of vengeance have urged him to seek the means of emancipating the race from which he was descended?

Taking advantage, then, of one of those terrible famines which ravage Egypt on failure of the fertilising inundations of the Nile, or of one of those destroying scourges of plague or typhus, which are not rare in those countries, he presented himself before the reigning prince as a celestial messenger, and, attributing those affections to divine wrath, succeeded in extorting from him permission to withdraw the Hebrew from their unhappy lot.

I would rather incline, however, to consider the revolt and

flight of the Hebrews as a revolution, long prepared by Moses and his brother Aaron, who seconded all his projects, and which the Egyptians did not perceive until too late to repress it.

As to the destruction of Pharaoh and his whole army in the waters of the Red Sea, I consign it, together with the passage of the fugitives dry-shod through that sea, to the apocryphal domain of miracle and invention.

We can imagine that Moses, who wrote all these things, after the fact, having described himself as a messenger of God, desired to surround them with a mysterious halo, very favourable, withal, to the accomplishment of his mission.

It was by the supernatural and the wonderful, that all his predecessors had imposed themselves upon the rude and superstitious masses; and like the clever man he was, his aim was to invest his power with a divine prestige that it might be less questioned.

Certainly it would not be easy task to conduct through deserts, in search of a fertile soil to receive and nourish them, these undisciplined hordes, who, slaves yesterday, free to-day would submit with difficulty, to any new control imposed upon them.

The desert was immense, where to go nobody knew, and Moses, no more than others. A programme, however, was necessary to appease the murmurs which daily became more menacing. "We are going to conquer the promised land," proclaimed Moses, and they continued their march.

Days, months, years pass away, and the wandering horde is still unable to escape from the sands. Now they go forward, stamping the earth with rage, then they retrace their steps; the outcasts become weary, they regret the land of Egypt, and blaspheme the God of whom Moses had made himself the interpreter. They remember the Ox Apis, which they had formerly seen carried in procession by the priests, with song and dance; they make one, of gold or of brass, with the bracelets of the women and the bucklers of the men, and they worship it, beseeching it to put an end to the sufferings they had no longer the courage to endure.

And Moses was invisible, alone in his tent;- perhaps he, too, was in despair.

All at once, at the decline of the day, the heavens became darkened, lightings flash through space, and the thunder's voice resounds.

It was the moment to act. The multitude heard with terror the manifestations of these physical phenomena which they could not understand. Promptly the chief appeared, his face expressive of inspiration; even before he had spoken, respect and submission were restored; he broke the idols, and, with a trumpet voice, announced that the wrath of Heaven, to punish their murmurs and their little faith, condemned them still to wander, before reaching the country of their hopes. And they continued to wander. It was time gained.

They came at last to a mountain-top from which they perceived vast plains covered with verdure. It was time; worn out with strife and fatigue, arrived at the term of his existence, Moses could but cry aloud, "Behold the land to which the Lord commanded me to conduct you!" He stretched forth his arms as if to take possession — and he died, leaving to his brother and to the faithful whom he had prepared, the duty of completing his work.

During his long wanderings he had written a book of the law, in which, assigning a fabulous past to these people of yesterday, and inspired by the traditions and sacred books which he had studied in Egypt, he revives the Indian legends on God and Creation, institutes priests or Levites, prescribes *yajñas* and their manner, and, in a few civil and religious laws, lays the foundation of the new society, which his successors were about to construct.

It is thus that, stripped of prodigy and fable, rejecting, above all, the unworthy role assigned by Moses to the Divinity for the success of his projects, I admit the historic tradition of the flight of the Hebrews, and of their arrival in the country they were to conquer.

Is not that, moreover, the very simple legend that might apply to all antique emigrations, to the cradle of all ancient civilisations?

Everywhere you find a legislator, a man who claims to be sent from God, and who succeeds in uniting and controlling the masses by the double prestige of his genius and his self attributed origin. Thus did, Manes, and Zoroaster impose their authority and establish their missions.

Will it be said that I substitute fable for fable? No, for I do but take the most salient points of primitive Hebrew history, which, alone, as appears to me, ought to be considered authentic, repudiating only the mysterious and the revealed, as I repudiate it in India, in Egypt, in Persia, in Greece, and in at Rome; claiming no right to admit the poetic and sacred legends of one, and to reject those of another.

What constitute the unimpeachable force of my reasoning is this unity, this identity of role of all the first founders of nations, basing their ascendancy on the religious idea; which. it must be admitted, is that which takes firmest hold of the naive intelligence of primitive peoples. Each attributes to God his book of the law – each legislates for religious as well as for civil life. All divide the people into castes, and proclaim the Superiority of the priest. Lastly, all, whether first claiming incarnation, or simple mission from God, are careful to envelope their death, as well as their birth, in mystery.

India is ignorant what was the end of Manu.

China, Tibet, and Japan translate Buddha to heaven.

Zoroaster was carried off by a ray of the sun.

And Moses, conveyed by an angle to the valley of Moab, disappeared from the eyes of his people, who knew not in what corner of the earth reposed his remains; and the belief prevails that he returned to God, who sent him.

This is all that sound reason can say about Moses. I have said that the role attributed to God by this legislator was unworthy of the majesty and grandeur of the Supreme Being. A truth which will be sufficiently established by reading the titles of different chapters of the Bible.

[Edition of Pere de Carrieres, of the Society of Jesus. Those who can read with reverence, or without disgust, the quotations of the author from the Jesuists' Bible, will find them nearly identical in our own Bible---Exodus, chapters vii. to xii., both inclusive. While we (translator) echo the author's peremptory.]

Halte la! The heart swells with disgust and indignation at review of such superstitions and such turpitudes!

Certainly, if I had not long time since abjured all partisanship, all narrow beliefs, the perusal of these absurdities would itself suffice to lead me to the worship of purification, which gives me conceptions of the divinity at once so simple and so sublime.

Do you see this God manifesting his power by invasions of frogs and of little tiles, then striking a whole people with plague and frightful ulcers, and at last by the massacre of all the first born of each family!

What a gradation from the ridiculous to the horrible!

Ah! you may search into all ancient mythologies, dive into all the mysteries of the Olympuses, explore the most obscure traditions of all the peoples, and I defy you to find anything so deplorable, so profoundly demoralising; and I dare defiantly to say, that if obliged to choose between the God of Moses and the Bull Apis. the Bull should be my God!

When he has well decimated Egypt by all sorts of scourges, Jehovah crowns his work by a revolting slaughter of children. But, it is not yet enough; he commands his people to preserve an eternal souvenir of this high fact, and to celebrate its anniversary as a festival with ceremonies and songs.

And the modern spirit still feeds upon such atrocities!

I already hear sacerdotalism denounce me as madman and blasphemer!

Who, then, is the madman? who the blasphemer?

Who makes God to wallow in a litter of blood!

Or, who refuses to see a butcher in the omnipotent, the omniscient, and the perfect?

This fanatic slave, brought up on charity at the court of Pharaoh, must have been well aware of the degradation and stupidity of the people whom he had emancipated, to have dared, when, after the fact, writing his history of this revolution, to surround it with these ridiculous horrors.

This is reality of Moses. He found it nowhere to copy. When presently showing that Biblical traditions are but falsified and ill-executed copies from the sacred books of the India, we shall have occasion to see that those people, far from making of God a bugbear, rejoiced to consider benignity and pardon the most beautiful attributes of His power.

It was indeed a people of parias that Moses led into the desert!

But yesterday, still subdued to the yoke, and stupefied by servitude, they but saw in the gods of Egypt the dark spirits of evil, who rejoiced in the sufferings and lamentations of their victims, so taught by their high caste rulers. **The Hebrew people became free without comprehending liberty; and Moses, the better to control them, made of his book a strange compound of pure Vedic studies under the priests, and traditions of the vulgar worship of the Egyptians.**

To sway a nation always ready to resume its old beliefs in the bull Apis, and the Golden Calf, and to enforce acceptance of the one God he proclaimed, it was necessary to assign him the same role as the gods of the past.

And were not prodigy and terror equally necessary to the forward impulsion of this servile horde, whom nothing in the past united as a nation, unless the remembrance of common suffering?

Moses might have seen the difficulty of his enterprise, when one day, in the country of Pharaoh, seeing two Hebrews quarrelling, he said to the aggressor---"Why do you thus abuse your brother?"

And that he was answered: "Who made you a prince and a judge over us? Would you kill me, as you killed and Egyptian yesterday?

From this moment, he, doubtless, perceived that the escape he meditated would be the easiest part of his programme to civilise this horde of outcasts, slaves and vagabonds.

Only thus can I account for his creation of the destroyer Jehovah, who but manifests himself by menace and vengeance -- a salutary curb imposed upon license and murmuring discontent.

But, if I understand it as a means at the debut of a nation, originating in servile insurrection, I understand it no farther nor can admit it as an after belief; enrolling it with all the other myths, all the other bugbears employed by the founders of antique societies.

Let us hear no more, then, of the people of God!

In surrounding their fabulous origin with murders and rapine (for, always, by God's command! they spoil Egyptians to the almost, by borrowing their vessels of gold and vestments!) the Hebrews cannot alter the judgement I have expressed of them, as nothing else than revolted parias. Apart from the arguments which I have developed, I find one in the Bible, itself, which I may call irrefutable, unless in these studies o the past, the true is only to be estimated by the absurd.

According to Jewish chronology, it was in the year 2298,

that Jacob went to establish himself in Egypt, with his whole family of seventy persons, sons, grandsons, and great-grandsons.

Then, by the same authority, it was in 2513, that is, two hundred and fifteen years after, that the Hebrews quit Egypt to the number of six hundred thousand men, *without counting women and children,* which should make a nation of at least two millions of souls.

Is it possible for an instant to maintain that within this short period, and in spite of the hardships to which they were subjected, to descendants of **Jacob** could have multiplied at this rate, and would it not be an outrage upon common sense to attempt establishing the truth of this legend?

The histories of the patriarchs and of Joseph are either fictions invented by Moses, or as I prefer thinking, old Egyptian traditions, picked up by this legislator and employed by him to make it appear that the providential mission of the Hebrews was of old date, and that their ancestors had already been the chosen of the Lord.

I ask it, in entire good faith, ought not a free, intelligent, historic criticism to reject this mass of prodigies and monstrous superstitions, which encumber the origin of the Hebrew nation.

We have repudiated Greek and Roman mythologies with disdain.

Why, then, admit with respect the mythology of the Jews?

Ought the miracles of Jehovah to impress us more than those of Jupiter?

It is possible to discover Supreme Wisdom, the God revealed to us by conscience, in either one or the other of these irascible sanguinary beings, prompt to vengeance the bugbears of popular credulity?

And, then, what is this role of pride and effrontery, unique in history?

A nation boasts itself the only people of God, exhibits to its neighbours only the most odious examples of duplicity and cruelty, and in God's name exterminates the occupants of lands which they desire to seize for themselves!

But yesterday slaves themselves, will they abolish slavery in their new community? No, and it is still in the name of the divinity, that they reduce to slavery the peoples whom they have conquered!

I know no people of the past so consistent in hypocrisy, or who better knew how to sanctify their means to their end.

Let not that surprise us, however. At the head of this theocracy established by Moses, appears the priest, the Levite, faithful to the ancient priestly role of subjugation by demoralisation;- this heir of Hindu Brahmanism continued, as in Egypt and in Persia, as in all primitive societies, to make of the Supreme being the instrument of his despotic desires, to utilise the religious idea for subjection of the credulous to the arbitrary influence of his caste.

When we shall have proven by examination into all its details, that this Hebrew social system, was also but a copy of that of Manu, will it not be evident, that Moses could only have been the inheritor, through Manes the Egyptian, of that legislator, and that, like his civil institutions, his Genesis was also a bequest from ancient India?

Thanks to researches already made on other people of the ancient world, we may say that this opinion is no longer a paradox; it is but the logical and consistent continuation of that **great movement by emigrations from the plateau of the Himalayas, whose influence extended to the four quarters of the globe, and from which it is natural to suppose that the Israelites, issuing from Egypt, could not escape.**

We shall establish this as a truth, in comparing the work of the Hebrew with that of the Indian legislator, and, the ground thus cleared, we may without fear consider the world's beginning, according to the Vedas, and the written traditions of the Indians which the Bible has but reproduced with very slight modifications.

One word more.

It appears to me not without interest to collate the opinions with which reason and research on the ancient societies of the world inspire me, with the appreciation by the Society of Jesus, of this tissue of cruelties and impostures.

I read in the advertisement at the head of the book of Exodus by the Father de Carrieres:

"Thus do Christians learn from this great Apostle (St. Paul) to reverence the profound judgements of God, in the obstinacy to which he abandoned Pharaoh, and to admire the infinite wisdom with which he made the obduracy of that prince in daring to resist him, subserve the manifestation of his glory and his power."

"The same Apostle further teaches them to consider the passage of the Red Sea, as typical of their baptism; the manna that fell from heaven as symbolic of the Eucharist; the rock from which issued the water that followed the Israelites in the desert, as the figure of Jesus Christ who nourished Christians in this life, and follows them in spirit and peace, until they have reached the true land of promise; Mount Sinai is an image of the earthly Jerusalem. The law, as an instructor, which could not teach true justice, but which led to Jesus Christ as its source; the shining glory of the face of Moses, as an image of that of the Gospel. The veil with which he hid himself, as a figure of the blindness of the Jews. The tabernacle, a type of the celestial sanctuary; the blood of victims as pre-figuring that of Jesus Christ."

Thus, it is always for the greater glory of God, according to our modern Levities, that Egypt was decimated by all sorts of scourges, plague, and slaughter!

No doubt the sanguinary mediaeval hecatombs and faggots were equally for the manifestation of celestial power; and the Vandois, and the victims of St. Bartholomew were pre-figured by the obdurate Egyptians!

What aberration? What perversion of all moral intelligence! It is profoundly painful to think that we are still obliged to discuss such superstitions, and that four or five thousand years of ruin have not led the peoples into the way of free thought and religious independence!

Let us courageously tear away their mask, and show to all that they are only the work of human weakness and human passions.

III

MOSES FOUNDS HEBREW SOCIETY ON THE MODEL OF THOSE OF EGYPT AND OF INDIA

In laying the foundation of his religious and political institutions, Moses did not escape that influence which we have described as pervading the ancient world.

Having led this horde of outcasts into the desert, followers according to the Bible, by a mixed multitude, it became necessary to discipline and give them laws, and accustom them to regular habits. The caste idea was too deeply rooted in their usage to be ignored, and it accordingly prevailed in the constitution of the new Government, which was nothing else than an exact reproduction of Indian social system.

Instead of four, there were twelve castes, of which the first was, as always, that of the priest, charged with all the functions, civil and religious, of the nation, interpreter of the world of God, guardian of the temples, alone permitted to sacrifice, sole judge of the sins of conscience, and of crimes committed against society.

For supreme head, this theocracy had a high priest, a potent and mysterious authority, that none might resist, whose word was law, both in the spiritual and the temporal, and who was only subject to the judgement of God.

It is the ideal of which Ultramontanism dreams to-day, the authority it would establish for the benefit of popes, by reducing modern societies to mere corporations, whose every thought and will should find at Rome, its law and its sovereign inspiration.

Will it be said that the Hebrew tribes were not castes, and that these were the natural division of their origin and descent from the sons of Jacob?

This filiations is to me but an ingenious fiction by Moses,

to enforce the divisions he established, as created by God himself, and against which the people would without doubt have murmured. Was it not, moreover, necessary thus to introduce imitations of a past, that reminded the Hebrews of their sufferings under Egyptian despotism, that nevertheless, no man should be tempted to change his tribe?

No sooner free than, always with the same design, the Hebrew legislator surrounds himself with initiated associates in his projects and his ambition, consecrates them priests, and places them under Divine protection, that the people may not be tempted to question the legitimacy of their authority.

These exclusive tribes or castes, like those of Egypt and India, were doubtless adopted by Moses, to establish forever the supremacy of the Levitie, and for the preservation of this family from all intermarriage with the other tribes.

At an epoch when all peoples had adopted the principle of government by the priest, what more simple than that Moses should confine himself to copying, with modifications, the situation of Indian emigrations and colonisations, honoured in Egypt and throughout Asia?

All this needs explanation of a Divine Mission, and belief in the fables and prodigies employed by the Hebrew legislator more easily to control the turbulent and heterogeneous horde under his command. Murmurs, disobedience, revolts were so frequent, that we ask how he could possibly have succeeded, had he not skilfully invented this God, always in the breach, slaughtering blasphemers and mutineers, and terrifying the mob by his atrocities of vengeance? Was it not in the name of Jehovah that twenty-three thousand Israelites were massacred by the tribe of Levi, that is, by the priests, after the schism of the golden calf? Whatever the energy of Moses, admitting these frightful scenes of carnage, they must have ended in his own death had he not divided the people into different classes, and above all, fanaticized the class of priests, who were of his tribe, and his most ardent supporters. For my own part, I can see no difference between Mediaeval Indian Brahminism and

Levitism, and every thing seems to proclaim the one descended from the other.

In connecting these two civilisations by their usage, we shall presently have occasion to show that the filiation is not imaginary, not merely a resemblance of institutions.

To Moses is assigned the honour of having been the first to establish, without obscurity, the grand idea of the Unity of God, which the nations, his contemporaries, do not, at least in the historic traditions of the epoch, appear to have as perfectly conceived. This opinion is an error which we shall have little trouble in refuting, although it has been consecrated by time and the Christian dogma, which, in accepting the Hebrew succession, would naturally adopt and propagate it with ardour.

Moses, initiated by his sacerdotal education in Egypt, in the splendours of Indian deism, instead of constructing for the Hebrews a worship based on the superstitions to which the Egyptian priests, with an obvious object, had habituated the lower castes, was the first to reveal to them the mysteries of initiation based upon the Unity of God, and the traditions of Creation, exclusively reserved by India and by Egypt, for the privileged castes of Brahmins and of hierophants.

But it is worthy of remark, that even in revealing to the masses these sublime notions on the Unity of the Supreme Being, he did not dare to present them in all their purity to this people, born of servitude, void of intelligence, and not sufficiently free of the past to permit separation for them, of the idea of God-creator, almighty, and benevolent, from all accessory ideas of cruel vengeance and terrible chastisements.

Hence it was that Moses dared not make his Jehovah preside over the worlds with that aspect, serene and calm, of the Indian sacred books, which so well becomes Majesty divine.

If on one side he had the merit, beyond his precursors, of daring in face of the nation, to proclaim the unity of God, and to prescribe the superstitions which Manu and Manes thought good enough for the people; on the other, making a retrograde step, he was forced, for the security of his power, and of the institutions he was founding, to make of that God a cruel being, fit to inspire terror and to command blind obedience.

The crowd of terrors and terrible manifestations, which other had infinitely divided by multiplicity of idols, Moses made to emanate from one alone; and his worship was neither less sombre, nor less sanguinary, than that of others. It is not Jehovah who commands all the massacres of the Bible, all the hecatombs of idolatrous nations, for the glorification of his name, and to clear the way for the quondam slaves of Egypt?

Respect for the horrible must be riveted in the soul,---love of the stupid struggle of intolerance, deeply rooted, to see in Moses ought else than a rude projector, whose chief allies were fire and sword, and in Jehovah ought else than a bugbear, a means of domination, placed at the service of a Sacerdotal oligarchy.

In short the government established by Moses was theocratic under the sovereign impulsion of the priests. The divisions of tribes which he ordained were castes designated to maintain the people in a state of stability suitable to assure success to the new power and new institutions. And we may, therefore, say that the Hebrews were, neither by their beliefs nor by their social state, an exception to the rule which pervaded all the people of antiquity.

Some take their stand on the sublimity of the Decalogue, to invest the Hebrews with a halo of morality, which they deny their contemporaries.

The Decalogue commands to honour father and mother, not to kill, not to commit adultery, not to steal, not to bear false witness against neighbours, and, lastly, to covet nothing that belongs to another.

These principles do not date from Mount Sinai; they are anterior to the Hebrews, and to all the civilisations that preceded them; and when Moses came to reveal them to the people on the mountain, conscience had of itself long made them known to all honest men. This Decalogue, proclaimed with so much pomp to the Hebrews midst thunders and sounds of trumpets, appears to me, moreover, a very bitter sarcasm. To read the Bible suffices to show that few people were more corrupt, few practised more duplicity in their relations with their neighbours, and that, lastly, few had less respect for the property of others.

They pick the pockets of Egypt before leaving it, traverse the desert, continue their brigandage, their violent spoliation on each new soil they tread, until exhausting the patience of people they are vigorously chastised and again reduced to servitude.

Except Moses and his successors, the parias remained parias; it was impossible to convert these quondam slaves of Pharaoh into a respectable people attached to the soil and inclined to work. Vagrants they began, and vagrants continued, despite their encampment in Palestine, and the nations, their neighbours, appear to have united, by common consent, to chastise and repulse their ever-recurring aggressions.

It is totally different society from this that will present itself to us in the India of the Vedas, in the India of primitive sacred traditions; and if the vulgar verities of the Decalogue are admired, with what sentiment shall we view those grand philosophic and moral principles which the Christian reformer came afterwards to revive to a world that had forgotten them!

That Moses knew them, studied them, doubtless, in his youth, seems proven by his avowal of the unity of the Supreme Being, as well as by his Genesis, which is but an echo of the Indian Genesis. And if he was incompetent to his task of regeneration, if he adopted Brahmanism rather than Vedism, perhaps we ought to attribute it to the degraded moral condition of the Hebrews in Egypt, whom independence had not changed, and which perhaps forced the legislature to govern, as we have said, by superstition and fear of the vengeance of a pitiless God.

With a different people to handle, possibly he might have constructed in Judea a society comparable with that of the best times of Greece.

It was perhaps not the man, therefore, that was incompetent, but the people, who wanted intelligence to understand him.

This seems so true, I believe so firmly, that the reform of Moses might have taken another stamp with a people less stupefied by servitude, that manifestly, the God of Genesis the God of early Biblical action, does not resemble the jealous Jehovah, a thirst for human sacrifice, of Exodus and following books.

We should say that as murmurs and opposition became more frequent in the desert, Moses felt the necessity of giving to the Divinity a more threatening aspect, to control and calm this horde, with whom the language of reason was powerless.

What would the God of the Vedas have done here, with his inexhaustible forbearance and forgiveness? This congregation of slaves and vagabonds would have banished him. They required an iron-handed God, to chastise-to exterminate twenty or thirty thousand men for an imprecation, a blasphemy, or a prayer to the Golden Calf.

And this is why Moses abandoned the Vedas, after Genesis, to devote himself, heart and soul, to Brahmanism, that is to domination by the priest and for the priest.

To some, doubtless, these opinions will appear very strange, for certainly our education of nineteen centuries does not predispose us either to exercise freedom of thought or to suffer freedom of speech!

Obliged, as we are, on one side to admit certain religious fictions which we may not discuss, and on the other to reject, on no better grounds, other religious fictions, which may we may but discuss, to deny. What can result from such a situation?

Truth here, i.e., with us–error there, i.e. with others: such is the rule of all parties, the system of all communions.

I perfectly understand that a free-thinker who has the courage to say, "I come to prove to you that all superstitions, like all despotism, have a common origin, and to indicate the fabric to be demolished, that you may construct a future from lessons of the past; I come to show you that there can be no possible composition with certain things in face of the ruin they have produced;" this would be pioneer, I perfectly understand, may be reviled and execrated like all those whose courageous course he follows, and whose works were cast into the fire, it being no longer permitted to dispose of persons.

IV

HEBREW PENAL SYSTEM

The penal system inaugurated by Moses was not exactly that of Egypt or of India; but the differences we discover, far from affecting the origin which we have assigned the Israelites, strikingly prove that very origin.

Moses, like his predecessors, as means of repression and expiation, ordains--

Death,

The bastonade

Fine,

And purification by sacrifice. (*yajña* was translated as sacrifice)

But he rejected all exclusion, partial and complete, from tribe or caste. a penalty which we have seen had been adopted by Persia, Greece, and Rome, and which with the laws of Justinian, passed afterwards into modern codes, under the name of civil death.

This refusal of Judaism to permit the interdiction of water and fire to great criminals although so consistent with Easter usage, is an exception which logically explains itself.

There is in this neither progress nor dream of humanity, for exclusion from caste or tribe would certainly have been better than the massacre of the twenty thousand Israelites, guilty only of having flirted with the daughters of Moab. And it needs but to read the Bible to see that it is full of hecatombs and human sacrifices, and the book itself is written with blood.

We cannot, then, here see any softening of ancient manners.

The thought that guided Moses, is too simple not to be true, and we may say, it was imperative on the situation.

If the Hebrew people, as we have shown consisted of the refuse of Egypt's criminals, if they were the parias of society under the Pharaohs, it became a necessity that Moses should not create parias in Hebrew society.

First, it was necessary that the new people should not be allowed to perceive a possibility that under any circumstances they could return to the miserable condition from which they had just escaped.

Then there was a reason of state, doubtless perceived by Moses, which was, not to create, by this caste exclusion, a nation within a nation, which gradually increasing might in time become a social danger.

The Egyptians had tried to arrest Israelite development by massacres and hardship: it was a wise policy to foresee that the same cause might some day enforce the same measures, from fear of servile revolution. The adoption, then, of this ancient penalty, tending infallibly to threaten the future with ferment and decomposition, Moses preferred the massacre *emasse* of all great criminals. Thus did they free themselves from those who denied Jehovah, as from those who murmured against the authority of the legislator, and the priests his successors.

For offences of minor importance, not essentially affecting the theoretic constitution of the Government, the *lex talionis* was established; an eye for an eye, a tooth for a tooth, etc. Vide Exodus, Chap. xxi. 24-25

Hail! this *first* appearance in ancient societies of the bar batous *lex talionis!*

What theocratic India and Egypt were incapable of inventing; what Manu, Zoroaster, and Manes, would have repelled with horror, it remained for Judaism and Jehovah to afford us.

This was no imitation, and Moses may claim the *lex*

talionis, as an original flower in his chaplet of legislator!

This penalty afterwards appears at the debut of many nations, but only in their primitive customs; no people but Israel, dared preserve it in their written laws.

The more we advance, the more shall we have occasion to repeat, that if Judea modified anything in the civilisation bequeathed by India and Egypt, it was but in the way of return to the barbarism and cruelty of early ages, when Nomad-Man, recognised no right but that of force.

"Leave the land to me, or I slay thee," says Cain to Abel.

"Submissive obedience to the Word of God, or death," says Moses to the Hebrews; who, in their turn, say to the neighbouring people, "Deliver up your wealth, your virgin daughters, and your houses, or you shall be destroyed with fire and sword."

I cannot forego a few lines, in detail, of all the massacres and all the bloodshed accomplished under the orders of Jehovah, whether by Moses and his successors upon the Israelites themselves, or by them upon the people whom they desired to despoil.

It will be no digression from my subject for, apart from the high moral and religious instruction it will afford, I shall thence also derive a triumphant argument against these who will not fail to deny the authority of Indian sacred books- to represent them as copied from the Bible.

The sublime traditions on the Unity of God, the Trinity, Creation, original transgression, and redemption, produced in India, a high philosophic and moral civilisation.

The copy of these traditions, which were not indigenous on Hebrew soil, could not regenerate people, who, begotten of rapine and murder, only knew how to live by murder and rapine.

V

EXAMPLES OF INDIAN INFLUENCE ON
HEBREW SOCIETY THROUGH EGYPT

MARRIAGE SYSTEM

The manners and customs of Judea so strongly recall those of India, as of themselves to remove all doubt that might remain as to the colonisation of the ancient world by emigrations from India.

We have seen the great characteristics of that old civilisation pervade Egypt, Persia, Greece, and Rome. Judea is now about to exhibit the same influence, even in the most minute details of its social organisation.

There needs no careful selection from the many points of contact and striking resemblances, that justify our still more confident assertion of that unity of origin of all the peoples of antiquity, which we have propounded from all first pages, as lincost an axiom.

Marriage of Hebrew and Hindu widows:

We read in Biblical Genesis:

Juda took for He, his first-born son, a wife named Thamar, He was wicked in the sight of the Lord, and the Lord slew him.

"Juda then said to Onan, his second son, marry Thamar, thy brother's wife, and raise up seed unto thy brother.

"But Onan, knowing that the children would not be his, but be accounted his bother's - *semen fundebat in terram.*"

Again we read in the book of Ruth:

"Boaz said: I take Ruth, the Moabitess, wife of Mahlon, to be my wife, to raise up the name of the dead in his inheritance, that his name be not lost in his family, among his brethren, and among his people.

Many other passages of the Bible show that it was a law, that the nearest relative of a man dying without issue should marry the widow, their progeny being considered children of the defunct, and dividing his inheritance.

Whence this custom, and what the rationale of the obligation imposed by the legislator? We have searched all the books of the Old Testament in vain; they throw no light on the subject. Most commentators, accepting the motive assigned by Boaz for his marriage with Ruth, believe that the union of the widow with the brother or relation of her deceased husband, had, in fact, no other object than to continue the race of the latter.

This conclusion is not satisfactory. Was the interest of a particular man, no longer in existence, of such importance, that a brother, or, in his default, a relative, should be required for his sake to forego his own name and race?

Ought not the brother or relative equally to desire progeny? Wherefore, then, compel them to marriage, which, in continuing the family of another, must terminate their own?

This custom, of which Judaism can give us no explanation had its origin in the religious beliefs of the Hindus, introduced into Egypt by emigration, and was adopted by the Hebrews, probably in ignorance of its purport.

As per Paurāṇika Hindu concept, a father can only attain the abodes of the blessed through expiatory sacrifices and funereal ceremonies, performed by his son, on his death, and renewed on each anniversary of his death. These sacrifices remove the last stains which prevent the soul's re-absorption into the Divine Essence, the supreme felicity provided for the just.

It is, therefore, a first necessity that every man should have a son who may open to him the gates of the immortal abode of Brahmā; and it is for this that Indian society makes its appeal to the devotion of brother or kinsman, stigmatising as infamous the refusal to perform so sacred a duty.

With the Hebrews all the sons of the widow belong to the dead husband, which is absurd seeing that, to continue the race of one, it extinguishes that of another.

With the Hindu, on the contrary, only the first son thus born belongs to the dead husband of his mother, becomes his heir, and is bound to accomplish the required funereal ceremonies. All other children are recognised as progeny of the brother or relative who has married the widow, and, in this way, his devotion does not ruin his own hopes. If no second son should be born to him, the law permits his adoption of one who shall bear his name, and perform his funereal sacrifices.

The Hebrew custom is mere meaningless, seeing that it assigns all the children born of the widow, to the defunct, taking no thought for the natural father whom it deprives of posterity.

The Hindu usage is rational and logical, seeing that it protects the interests of both, and also assigns a religious motive for an act otherwise incomprehensible. Whereas the Bible makes no attempt at explanatory justification, which it would, probably, have been puzzled to invent.

We see clearly that it is but a preserved Hindu tradition, its legitimate object forgotten. And Onan would not, certainly have dreamt of prolonging the sterility of Thamar, had the law assigned to his brother only the first son born to him.

FORBIDDEN ANIMALS

Animals forbidden as impure by the Bible

Moses prohibits the use of all ruminant animals that divide not the hoof, and also the pig, which, although cloven-footed does not ruminate.

Of fishes he permits those with scales and fins, but forbids all others, as impure.

Of birds, the following are forbidden:

The eagle, the griffin, the falcon, the kite the vulture, and their species. The crow and its kind, the screech-owl, the ibis, the cormorant, the swan, the bustard, and the porphyrion. The heron, the stork, the lapwing, the bat, and all such as both fly and creep on fall fours.

Of land-animals, are prohibited as impure--

The weasel, the mouse, the crocodile, and their kinds. The musk-rat, the chameleon, the lizard, and the mole.

The man who eats of these animals, is impure, like them.

Who touches them, when dead, is impure until the evening.

The vessels that has contained them is defiled, and should be broken.

Forbidden by Brahmanical prohibitions.

The regenerated man shall abstain from quadrupeds that divide not the hoof, except those permitted by Scripture.

The domestic pig (not the wild bear) is declared impure, although dividing the hoof.

All birds of prey, without exception, such as the vulture, the eagle, the kite, all that strike with the beak and tear with the claws, are prohibited.

And it is especially remarkable that the same prohibition protects the sparrow, as destroyer of hurtful insects and preserver of the harvest.

Then the crane, the parrot, the swan, the woodpecker, and all that seize their prey with the tongue.

All fish that have not fins and scales.

Lastly, creeping animals, or that dig holes their claws are forbidden, as most impure of all.

All impurity from contact with dead animal matter continues for ten days and ten nights for four days, or only for one day, according to the individual's reputation for virtue and wisdom.

The vessel of brass, silver or gold, that has contained or simply touched impure matter, must be purified, as ordained.

The earthen vessel should be broken and deeply buried in the earth, for nothing can purify it.

What are we to say to such homologous legislation? Will it be objected that these prohibitions are but sanitary regulations, common to all Oriental people? Not the less would India appear the initiatrix, and to have led the way.

There is but one way to refute all this, and that is by denying the antiquity of India! I fully expect something of this kind from sworn champions of a certain class. I would beseech them to go a little farther, and prove the Sanskrit begotten of the Hebrew! The Hebrew parent of the Sanskrit! Who knows but I may really witness such a pleasantry!...

Ordea of Woman suspected of Adultery: We read in the Bible - (Book of Numbers):

" The husband shall bring his wife before the priest, and shall present for her on offering of a tenth part of a measure of barley-flour. He shall add no incense and pour no oil thereon, for it is a sacrifice of jealousy, an offering for the discovery of adultery.

"And the priest having taken some holy water in an earthen vessel, he shall therein put a little earth from the floor of the tabernacle, and shall say to the woman, 'If a man has not approached you, these bitter waters, charged with maledictions, will harm you not; but if you have been unfaithful to your husband, let your stomach swell and burst, and your thigh become rotten,' and he shall present her the draught."

We read in *Gautama- Dharmasūtra*:

"It was an ancient custom to bring the woman accused of admitting the embraces of another man than her husband to the gate of the pagoda and deliver her to the officiating priest, who having thrown a sprig of *causa*, with a little earth gathered from the foot-prints of an unclean animal, into a vessel of water drawn by a pariah, presented it to the woman to drink, saying-'If your womb has not received strange semen, this draught will be to you of ambrosial sweetness; If, on the contrary, you have been thus defiled, you will die, and you will be born again of a jackal; but in the meantime your body will be affected with elephantiasis and fall into rottenness.' For this religious rite the law of late," &c., &c.

"Who shall touch the body of a dead man is unclean for seven days, and must be cleansed by aspersion of the waters of expiation. **Defilement from contact of the Dead (Bible, Numbers)**

"All who enter the tent of the dead and all the vessels therein, are unclean for seven days. The defiled defiles all he touches." Defilement from contact of the Dead (Indian Tradition)

Impurity from touching the dead continues for ten days (Manu, lib.v.):

When a man dies, all the vessels in the house are impure. Vessels of metal are purified by fire, vessels of earth are broken and buried.

Man is cleansed by ablutions with the waters of purification.

Manu, who describe some of the forms and usage of purification in his time, in discussing such practices, exclaims, from a lofty standard unknown to the Bible:

"Of all things pure, purity in the acquisition of riches is the best; he who preserves his purity in becoming rich, is really pure, and not him who is purified with earth and water.

"Wise men purify themselves by forgiveness of offences, by alms, and by prayer.

"The learned purifies himself by study of the Holy Scripture. As the body is purified by water, so is the spirit by truth.

"Sound doctrines and good work purify the soul. The intelligence is purified by knowledge."

That this idea of defilement from the dead, extending ever to inanimate things, is another Indian legacy, cannot be doubted. Moses has copied these antique traditions word for word, but in reviving usages has been careful not to reproduce those wide views, those grand thoughts which we encounter at each step in Manu, whenever, forgetting his role of subservience to sacerdotalism, he echoes the sublime breathings of the Primitive and unabridged Vedas.

It is not the last time that the Bible will be found beneath, and never will it surpass, its model.

Pale reflex of that antique civilisation which inspired the old world, it would seem to have made it a rule only to initiate the new in the ridiculous superstitions with which Brahmanical sacerdotalism occupied the lives of the people, to make them forget their subjugation.

LEVITICAL SACRIFICES AND CEREMONIES BORROWED FROM HINDUS

The sacrifices and ceremonies ordained by Moses are borrowed in their minutest details from the India.

Gomedha is one of the *Śrauta Yajñas* in Vedic tradition aimed at the preparedness of Land for Agricultural purpose. Later on *Gomedha* was taken for a wrong meaning. *Go* in Veda signified earth or planets whereas in post Vedic Sanskrit this word was also applied to 'cow'. So the very meaning of Vedic *Gomedha* was wrongly taken by Indian immigrants to Egypt and Israel for or ox or its later conventional meaning 'Cow or ox sacrifice. (Editor)

Leviticus also ordains the immolation of an ox at the door of the tabernacle.

Leviticus, on the same pattern, ordains the sacrifice of sheep, of goats.

The Hindu fruit offering consists of flour, rice, oil, ghee, and fat of all kinds.

The Hebrew, for the same oblation employ flour, bread, and oil and the first fruits of all grains.

With both peoples, salt should be added to all offerings; and Indian priests and Levites alike divide among themselves portion of the sacrifice.

A perpetual fire named as *Gārhapatya Agni* is kept burning in the Vedic Alter.

The same fire burns in the Jewish tabernacle.

Lastly, in India as in Judea, all impurities and all offences against religion are atoned by *yajñas* and ceremonies of purification.

I will dwell no farther on this subject, what I have said appearing to me abundantly to establish imitation.

It is remarkable that, like Egypt, where it became a divinity their to the people like Persia an Greece, where it constituted most orthodox hecatomb; so did Judea, too, inherit this respect for the Ox, which is incontestably of Indian origin. Thus do we encounter at each page of the Bible such passages as these:

"You shall not muzzle the mouth of the ox that treads out the corn, and you shall permit him to eat thereof.

"You shall not plough with an ox and an ass yoked together.'

These evidences of respect, we must admit, are but the remains of ancient, traditions of the Egyptians inherited from India, from which Moses was unable wholly to emancipate himself.

Hindu and Hebrew purification of women after child birth

We read in Leviticus

"If a woman, suscepto semine brings forth a male child, she is impure for seven days, as for her menstrual period.

"If confined of a girl, she is impure for fourteen days, and her purification shall require sixty days.

"When the days of the purification are accomplished, whether for girl or boy, she shall, in testimony thereof, bring as an offering to the door of the Tabernacle, a lamb of a year, a young pigeon or a turtle dove, and give it to the priest, for an expiation."

And in Manu

"The birth of a child is a defilement to its parents, especially to the mother, who is declared impure for as many days as have elapsed months, since her conception, and her purification shall be accomplished, as after her natural seasons."

And We read in Kullka's Commentaries

Formerly, after ablutions, it was customary for the woman, in terminating her ceremonies of purification, to offer a young unshorn lamb, together with honey, rice, and ghee. At present, after ablutions, she but offers to priest, tex measures of rice, and six copas of clarified butter.

The possession of property forbidden to Brāhmaṇas

The Brahmin's mission, according to Manu, is to officiate at, *yajñas* and to teach the Holy Scriptures; he may not devote any portion of his time as consecrated to the Lord, to cultivation of the soil, herding of cattle, or gathering of harvests. These labours have been assigned to Vaiśyas there is not a field in India, a farm, a tree, or a domestic animal, but must contribute to satisfy the wants of the Lord's elect.

"Give to the Brahmins," says the divine Bhṛgu, "your firs-gathered measure of rice, the first calf, the first kid, the first lamb of your folds of each year; give them also the first fruits of your cocoa-trees, the first oil that flows from your press, the first piece of stuff that you weave; and finally, if you will that the Lord shall preserve to you your possessions, and that the earth shall produce abundantly, according to your desires, know that the first of all that belongs to you, belongs to them."

Identical Hebrew ordinance:

Jehovah by the mouth of Moses and Aaron, forbids any assignment of land to the Levites.

"I have given you," says Jehovah, "all that is most excellent of corn, wine, and oil-all that is offered as first fruits to the Lord.

"All the first fruits of the earth that are presented to the Lord, shall be reserved for your use; the pure of your household shall eat thereof.

"All that the children of Israel vow to me, shall be yours.

"All the first-born, whether of man or beast, that is offered to the Lord, shall belong to you; providing, nevertheless, that ye shall receive a price for the first-born of man, and shall exact redemption money for the unclean of animals.

"But ye shall not redeem the firstlings of the ox, the goat, and the sheep, for they are agreeable to the Lord."

The only difference between Indian and Hebrew, is, that the first-born of man was not, and the firstlings of unclean animals could not be offered to Brahmins.

Such an approach to identity scarce needs comment, the influence of India being palpable, both in detail and ensemble of the great principles bequeathed by her to social antiquity.

Levitical impurities and their purification:

When we read in the 15th chap. of Leviticus, the laws of purification for involuntary defilements of either man or woman, we are struck with very natural surprise at finding them a mere reproduction of Indian sacred ordinances on the same subject.

Let us take, for example, the two cases of the above mentioned chapter, and collate them with their Indian parallels.

Uncleanness of the man

"Speak unto the children of Israel, and say unto them, the man afflicted with seminal flux is unclean.

"And ye shall know he is thus afflicted, when a fœtid humour shall constantly gather and adhere to his skin.

"The bed whereon he sleeps, the seat whereon he sits, shall be defiled.

"If a man touches his bed, he shall wash his clothes and himself in water and remain unclean until the evening.

"Who shall have touched his person, etc. etc.

"Should he expectorate upon one that is pure, the latter, shall, remain impure until the evening.

"The saddle, and all that has been under the person so afflicted, shall be unclean until the evening. And who shall carry any of these things, shall wash and be unclean until the evening. And if, before so washing, he shall touch another man that other shall also wash, and be unclean until the evening.

"Any vessel touched by such man, if of earth, it shall be broken, if of wood, it shall be washed with water.

"Should the afflicted be healed, he shall yet count seven days, and having washed his person and his clothes in running water, he shall be clean.

"On the eighth day, he shall take two turtle-doves and two young pigeons, and shall present himself before the Lord at the entrance of the Tabernacle of the Covenant, and shall give them to priest who shall offer one for a sin, and the other for a burnt offering, and shall pity for him before the Lord that he be cleaned from his impurity.

"The man who shall have gone in into a women (*vir de quo egrditui itmen coitus*) shall wash his whole body, and be unclean until the evening.

"The woman whom be shall have gone in unto, shall in like manner wash, and be unclean until the evening."

Uncleanness of the Woman

"The woman in her menstrual state, shall be secluded for seven days."

"Who shall touch her shall be unclean until evening, and whatever she shall sleep upon, or sit upon, during the days of her seclusion, shall be defiled."

"Who shall have touched her bed, shall wash his clothes, and having plunged himself in water, shall be unclean until evening.

"If a man approach her while in this monthly recurring condition, he shall be unclean of seven days, and all the beds whereon he sleeps shall be defined."

"The woman in whom this condition is irregular, or prolonged beyond the natural period, shall remain unclean as for each month while it continues."

"And during this prolongation, all on which she shall have slept or sat shall be defiled, and whosoever shall have touched them shall wash his clothes and his person, and be unclean until the evening."

"The period over, and its effects having ceased, the woman shall count seven days before purifying herself."

"On the eighth she shall offer for herself to the priest, two turtle doves and two young pigeons, at the entrance of the tabernacle of the covenant."

"The priest shall offer one for a sin, and the other for a burnt offering, and shall play before the Lord for her, and for her purification."

"Ye shall, therefore, teach the children of Israel that they preserve themselves from all impure things, that they die not of such defilement, and pollute not any tabernacle which is in their midst.

"Such is the law for one afflicted with seminal flux, or who shall defile himself in approaching a woman."

"Such is also the law as regards the woman secluded during her monthly periods, or when that period recurs irregularly or so prolonged; and such also for the man who shall approach her at such a time."

Vedic Impurities and Purification (Ramatsariar)

The Vedas, or Holy Scriptures, propound the principle, that as spiritual tarnish is atoned by prayer and good works, so should personal defilement be purified by ablutions.

Ramatsariar, whom we are about to cite, is a sage of high antiquity, greatly venerated by Brahmin theologians in the south of India, and a recognised authority on all connected with the ceremonies and sacrifices of religion.

His words on the subject are:

"Men and women are alike subject to a condition that forbids their participation in family festivals and ceremonies of the temple, for they are unclean, nor are they purified by ablutions in the sacred waters of the Ganges until after that condition has ceased."

Uncleanness of the Man

"Every man who has contracted disease from the use or abuse of women shall be impure while it continues, and for ten days and ten nights after his restoration."

"His breath is impure, his saliva and his perspiration are impure."

"He may not eat with his wife, with his children, nor with any other of his caste or relations, his food becomes unclean, and all who eat with him are unclean for three days."

"His clothes are defiled, and must be cleaned by the waters

of purification, and all who touch him are unclean for three days."

"Who speaks to him from the leeward is impure, and purifies himself by ablution at sunset."

"The matof his bed is defiled, and must be burned."

"His bed is defiled, and be cleaned by the waters, of purification."

His drinking vessels, and the earthen dishes that have contained his rice are defiled, and must be broken and buried in the earth."

"If his vessels are of copper or any other metal, they may be cleansed by the waters of purification, or by fire."

The woman who, knowing his condition, shall consent to him, shall be unclean for ten days and ten nights, and shall offer the sacrifice of purification after having bathed in the tank destined for shameful defilements.

"The man thus defiled shall be incapable of performing the anniversary funereal ceremonies of the death of his parents; the sacrifice would be impure, and rejected by the Lord."

"The horse the camel, the elephant on which he may ride on pilgrimages shall be impure, and shall be washed in water wherein is dissolved a spring of causa."

"If he makes a pilgrimage to the Ganges, his fault shall not be remitted, because he did it while unclean."

"If he brings back the water of the holy river, they may not serve for waters of purification, they become impure like himself."

"Should he in this state strike a man of his own caste, he shall suffer double the ordinary fine, and the man struck shall be impure until sunset."

"When healed, he shall wash himself in the pound for shameful defilements; he shall then perform his ablutions in the waters of purification, and thereafter devote the entire day to prayer, for which he has been disqualified until then."

"He shall make abundant offering to religious devotees."

"He shall then present himself at the gate of the temple, and shall there deposit his offerings of rice, of honey, and of ghee, with a young lamb that has not yet been shorn. If poor, and unable to offer a lamb, he shall offer "couple of young pigeons without spot, and which shall not yet have built nest or warbled the song of love."

"He shall then be purified, and may again rejoice with his wife and children."

Impurity of Woman

"The Manu has said- 'Sixteen complete days with four distinct days, interdicted by those of good repute, constitute what is called the natural season of the woman, during which her husband may approach her with love. Of these sixteen days, the first four being forbidden, as also the eleventh and the thirteenth, the remaining ten days are approved."

"The Veda has said, 'The husband should respect his wife during her natural seasons, as we respect the blossom of the banana which announces fecundity and future harvest."

"The eleventh and thirteenth days are interdicted from motives of continence. The first four days alone are considered defiling to those who do not respect them."

"During these four days the woman is impure; let her take refuge in her apartment, and hide herself from her husband, her children, and her servants."

"Her respiration, her saliva, and her perspiration are impure."

"What she touches becomes instantly impure, and the milk coagulates in the vessel which she hold in her hands."

"The mat of her bed is defiled, and shall be burnt, and the bed cleansed with the waters of purification."

"Whatever she may repose upon shall be impure, all who

shall touch her shall be impure, and shall purify them selves by evening ablutions.

"Let her not rub herself with saffron.

"Let her not dress herself with flowers.

"Let her not desire her women to dress her hair; in this state she should not seek to please."

"Let her lay side her jewels, for they will be defiled, and must be purified by fire."

"She should not eat with her husband, her children, or her women, even should the latter be of her own caste."

"Let her refrain from making offerings or assisting at funereal ceremonies; her offering will be impure, the ceremonies defiled."

"Should the four days' impurity, ordained by the divine Manu, be prolonged by two, by four, or by six days, purification may not be effected during such time, as the law prescribes."

"When all external signs have ceased, and after two ablutions of the morning and of the evening, which are called ablution of the rising and ablution of the setting sun, let her accomplish her cleansing with the water of purification."

"Let her then present herself at the gate of the pagoda, and deposit her offerings of rice, of honey, and of ghee; let her also offer a young lamb without spot and unshorn or in default a couple of pigeons that have not yet warbled the song of love, nor built their nests."

"And having done so she will be purified, and may resume her household occupations."

"And she may recall to her, her husband, who had separated himself in obedience to the word of Scripture, 'He who during the interdicted nights shall abstain from conjugal communing, preserves himself as pure as a *dvija* or a *Brahmācharī*.'"

With such striking parallels between Hebrew and Indian society before us, he must indeed be an unflinching champion of revelation to see in Moses ought but a legislator who, having to legislate for a people, the issue of a servile class, of a class that knew no subordination to other rules than those of labour and of endurance, was content to copy Manes, and those Egyptian institutions which are incontestably of Oriental origin.

Do we not know, moreover, that all the people of Asia were subject to the same usages, still honoured by the majority of them?

In those hot climates religion took upon itself the duty of sanitary legislation for personal cleanliness, as the only means of contending against deangerous epidemics that periodically desolate those countries, and guarding against leprosy, that hideous malady that Europe knows no more, but which still prevails in the East with the same virulence as in ancient times.

From Manu to Muhammad these sanitary laws were the same; climate indicated the necessity, and I certainly should not have taken the trouble to show that Moses was but the copyist of earlier usages, but which it was natural to adopt, were it not that there are people who, in their enthusiasm, whether sincere or conventional, obstinately persist in everywhere seeing revelation and the finger of God.

Moses commanded the sacrifice of an ox upon the altar, as a corrupt form of the Vedic *Gomedha*, the Hierophants of Egypt, the Magi of Persia, the priests of ancient Greece; instead of therein seeing the natural adoption of usages as old as the world, the Jesuits, Menochius, and Carriere, there find a type and symbol of the Eucharist!

Moses commands the ablution required by climate, and adopts the regulations ordained by Manes and Manu; instead of admitting that he has therein but followed the prevailing custom of the East, the same Jesuits see in the ablution imposed upon the Hebrews a symbol of the purity of the new faith, which should, later, regenerate the Christian world!

The system of interpretation is always the same, the most in significant custom is attributed to Mount Sinai, and to Divine inspiration. But to sustain such propositions, to what pitiable arguments are we not obliged to descend!

But why are we astonished? Have we not long known that for certain classes there is neither historic truth, good sense, nor reason, outside their own pale?

Will Brahmins, Magi Levites, and Hierophants, in proclaiming themselves the chosen of God, the sole dispensers of truth and right, for a moment permit discussion of their own position? Do they not proscribe their enemies? Have they not made monarchs tremble who sought emancipation from their rule? Have they not governed by torture and by the stake?

What ground for surprise, then, if we find the tradition continuous; if the heritage has found inheritors, and if modern Leviteism, gather all its forces, call out all its reserves for a pitched battle, with the avowed object of proscribing reason and liberty, and of revivifying that ancient sacerdotal despotism, which heretofore filled the world with ruins, and with martyrs?

Prohibition of the blood of animals as food And Prohibition of dead animals

We read in Leviticus: "If a man, whether of the house of Israel, or of the strangers that dwell amongst you, shall eat blood, the eye of my wrath shall rest upon him, and I will destroy him from amongst his people.

"Because the life of the flesh is in the blood, and I have given it to you that it may serve you at the altar, as an expiation for your souls, and that the soul be expiated by the blood."

"For this have I said to the children of Israel, that none amongst you nor of the strangers that dwell among you, shall eat blood."

"If any man of the children of Israel, or of the strangers amongst you, shall take any animal in the chase, or any bird in the net, that it is lawful to eat, let him spill the blood, and cover it with earth."

"For the life of all flesh is in the blood; and for this have I said to the children of Israel: 'The blood of all animals shall ye not eat, for the life of the flesh is in the blood, and who shall eat of it shall be punished with death.'"

"If any man of the children of Israel, or of strangers, shall eat of the flesh of any animal that shall have died, or shall have been killed by another animal, he shall wash his vestments and his person in water, and shall be impure until the evening, and shall be cleansed by this ceremony."

"But if he wash not his vestments and his person, he shall remain defiled."

Indian prohibitions on the same subject. We read in Ramatsariar:

"The man who eats of the blood of an animal permitted as food is called the son of a vampire, and shall perish, for no man should nourish himself with blood."

"Who shall eat of the blood of an animal forbidden, shall die of leprosy, and his soul shall revive in the body of an unclean jackal."

"The blood is the life, it is the Divine fluid that waters and fertilises the matter of which the body is formed, as the hundred arms of the Ganges water and fecundate the sacred soil; and as it would be senseless to attempt to dry up the source of the great river, so may not the sources of life be uselessly drained, nor profaned as food."

"It is through the blood that the Divine essence emitted from the Great All (who is all and is in all), and which is the soul, unites itself to the body. It is the blood unites the fœtus to the mother, it is by the blood we hold to God."

"We eat not sap of trees, which is their blood, and produces fruit. In like manner we may not eat blood of animals, which is their sap."

"The blood contains the mysterious secrets of existence, no created being can exist without it. To eat blood is to profane to Creator's Great Work."

"Let man who has eaten of it fear that in successive transmigration be may never escape from he body of the unclean animal in which his soul has been re-born."

"When you desire to eat of the flesh animals, clean and not forbidden, whether ruminants, and dividing the hoof, or others taken in the chase, fowls or quadrupeds, make a hole in the earth and cover it over, after having therein spilled the blood of the animal you would eat."

"Apart from pains of the other world, elephantiasis, leprosy, and diseases the most vile attend him who shall transgress these prohibition."

Prohibition of animals that have died

"The animal that dies naturally, or by accident is impure, although not of a class forbidden by the Holy Scripture, for the blood is still in the body, and has not been spilled on the earth."

"Who eats of it eats of the blood with the flesh, which is forbidden, and be becomes impure as the animal of which he has eaten."

"If so many of the lower classes die of leprosy, and of vile disease which make their bodies a prey to worms, even before they have ceased to live, it is because they feed upon every dead animal they find."

"Who shall have thus eaten should proceed to the tank for vile defilements, and having washed his clothes, plunge his body into the water, and after three prolonged ablutions, shall remain unclean until the second sun rising."

In forbidding blood as food, Moses assigns no other reason for the prohibition than that expressed in this line, "Because the life of the flesh is in the blood," and as usual offers no explanation of his idea.

We see plainly that he was addressing a people who required rather to be ruled, than taught, and who accepted his prohibitions without requiring a reason.

In India, on the contrary, the same prohibition requires to be developed, to address itself to the understanding, to make it understood why it was ordained, and then the attendant considerations assume a lofty import, which the Bible has not perceived, because its version was but an imperfect recollection:

"The blood is the life, it is the Divine fluid that waters and fecundates the matter of which is formed the body, as the hundred arms of the Ganges water and fertilise the sacred soil."

"It is through the blood that the pure essence emanating from the Great. Whole, and which is the soul, unites itself to the body."

Science may laugh at this definition of the Veda; the thinker will admire the emblem.

And Moses certainly but curtailed his recollections when he wrote this simple explanation of the law he imposed, "Because the life of the flesh is in the blood."

Do not these striking coincidences prove incontestably that the Bible is but an echo of Oriental institutions? I don't know if I delude myself, but it seems to me that, seriously considered, such is the conclusion that naturally presents itself from simple study of the book left by Moses.

In the five books attributed to this legislator, we find at each step details, manners, customs, ceremonies, modes of sacrifice, laws, which, given without the faintest explanation, can only find their *raison d'être* in imitation of ancient civilisations, and the farther we advance in this comparative study the more shall we become persuaded that Moses did but abridge, for the use of the Hebrews, those institutions of Egypt which the latter had received in their corrupt form India.

Israelites forbidden to kill their oxen, sheep, or goats elsewhere than before the tabernacle.

Thus says Leviticus:-

"And the Lord spake again unto Moses, and said unto him:

"Speak unto Aaron and to his sons and tell the children of Israel, 'Behold what the Lord hath commanded, behold what He hath said:

" 'Every man of the house of Israel who shall have killed an ox, a sheep, or a goat, in the camp or out of the camp, instead of slaughtering them before the tabernacle as offerings to the Lord, shall be guilty of murder, and shall perish in the midst of the people as if he had shed the blood of one of this fellows.'

"Therefore, should the children of Israel present to the priest their animals for slaughter, instead of slaughtering them in the fields, that they may be sanctified by the Lord, to whom they have been offered as a peace-sacrifice, before the Tabernacle of the Covenant."

"The priest shall sprinkle the blood upon the alter at the gate of the Tabernacle of the Covenant, and shall burn the fat for a sweet savour to the Lord."

"And thus shall they no more sacrifice their animals to demons, to whom they were before sacrificed, and this law shall be eternal for them and for their posterity."

"Say unto them: If a man of the house of Israel, or of those who have come from without, and who are strangers amongst you, kill an animal without bringing it to the entrance of the Tabernacle of the testimony that it may be sanctified by the Lord, he shall perish in the midst of his people."

Before investigating the symbolic meaning, of this curious injunction against the slaughter of animals, ox, lamb, or goat, except at the gate of the Tabernacle and in the hands of the priest, let us see what were the Indian ordinances on the subject:

We read in Manu lib.v:

"The Being who exists by his own will has himself created animals in course of the *Yajña* (process of creation) and by *Yajña* (process of creation) is this universe magnified, therefore the slaughtering is not permitted in *Yajña*."

"For as many hairs as had the animal on its body, so many times shall he who slaughter it perish by a violent death at each succeeding birth by transmigration.

"Who shall eat of the cooked meals bought or received from another, after having offered it to God, is not guilty, for to eat cooked meals after accomplishment of *Yajña* has been declared the divine law."

"A Brahmin should never eat meals which have not been consecrated by prayers, but let him eat conformably to the eternal law, after consecration by holy words."

"Who shall even daily nourish himself on the vegetation permitted for food, commits no fault, for Brahmā has created vegetation to be eaten and others to eat them."

"Let the devotee who knows the law never desire to destroy vegetation without making it an offering, let him never eat vegetation without conforming to this rule, unless under urgent necessity."

"Who merely for his pleasure shall destroy vegetation, his happiness shall not increase neither in life nor after death."

"But the anchorite in his forest retreat should never commit murder upon animals without sanction of the Veda, even under distress."

Extract from the *Sāmaveda*:

"We should respect animals, for their imperfection is the work of supreme wisdom that governs the world, and that wisdom ought to be respected even in its minutest works."

"You shall not, therefore, kill animals which are, like yourself, of divine creation."

"You shall not torment them."

"You shall not afflict them."

"You shall not over-work them."

"You shall not abandon them in their old age, remembering the services they have rendered you."

"Man may only use vegetation for food; carefully shunning those that are forbidden as unclean."

"Even in destroying vegetation for food he commits a fault, for which he will be severely punished if he observes not the prescribed rules."

"Let him take vegetation before the temple, and the priest shall offer a part of it to the *Yajña*, and he shall sprinkle the sap of the vegetation upon the altar.

"For the sap is the life, and life, in departing, should return to God."

"We shall eat without conforming to the prescribed rules of Holy Scripture shall die ignominiously, for he has destroyed it without offering it to the Master of all things."

On the same subject, Ramatsariar (Commentaries)

"Who would observe the prescribed law will not eat the flesh of animals."

"Who shall eat the flesh, shall be cursed in this world and in the next, for Manu has said, 'He shall devour me in the other world whose flesh I shall eat in this."

It appears from the above cited passages of Leviticus, that Moses prohibited the slaughter of animals by the Hebrews, elsewhere than at the gate of the Tabernacle, under penalty of death.

But, as usual, the legislator stoops not to explain his motives and the object of his prohibition.

Wherefore in the words of the Bible, forbid the slaughter of all animals in *castris vel extra castra,* in the camp, or outside of the camp?

Verse 7, chap. xvii, Leviticus, which treats of this matter, contains a semblance of explanation in these words: "*Et nequaquam ultra immolabunt hostias saus dæmonibus,* and they shall henceforth no more offer their sacrifices to false gods."

But what does this passage prove? It simply indicates that formerly the Israelites offered their sacrifices before statues of gods that Jehovah had overthrown, and the same custom was continued for the profit of the new worship.

What we wish to discover in the works of Moses is the idea that suggested this prohibition of immolation elsewhere than at the gate of the Tabernacle, *ut sanctificentur Domino,* that the slaughtered animal be sanctified by the Lord.

Moses did but abridge the ordinances of ancient Egypt borrow from India as suited to him, and in retaining the custom, always contrives (he is a careless transcriber) to forget the idea that gave it birth.

Let us return to the passages above transcribed from Manu and the Veda on the same subject, and then it is possible to dissipate the obscurity of the Bible-text, to explain it logically always deducing therefrom the natural conclusion that this text, like all the rest, is but the result of an ill-executed copy.

Veda says:

"The blood is the life, and all life in its extinction should return to God."

Hence the prohibition addressed by Manu and the Holy Scriptures to all devotees, and holy men, to eat of vegetation that has not been first offered to *Yajña*. The Bible copied the same statement with respect to animal eating.

"Every man of the house of Israel who shall have killed an ox, or a sheep, or a goat, in the camp or out of the camp, and who shall not have presented them at the gate of the Tabernacle to be offered to the Lord, shall be guilty of murder."

It was from the Indian (Vedic) tradition of not eating meals / vegetation without first offering them to the *Yajñiya* fire that the non-vegetarian East adopted this practice of sanctifying the flesh of which they were about to partake, by offering its blood (its life) to the Lord.

Later, this idea became dim and symbolic; and the custom of sacrificing each animal killed, to the Creator, ceased. For this daily usage was substituted periodical festivals, during which the people brought animals of all kinds to be sacrificed by the priest on the altar, for general purification.

Thus have all ancient civilisations proceeded from each other; and thus, in comparing their habitual usages in the most minute details of life do we discover that community of origin which, so far from being a paradoxical idea, is the inevitable and logical result of the laws which govern human development.

Catholic opinion, which persists in seeing in ancient Hebrew usages a type of the New Church, explains this chapter of leviticus in another manner.

According to it, these prohibitions were simply established by God, to prevent the Jews from offering sacrifices elsewhere than at the Tabernacle.

I would have it remarked, that the Bible employs this expression: *Homo qualibet de domo Israeli;* that is, any Israelite who shall have slaughtered an animal elsewhere than before the gate of the Tabernacle.

If a sacrifice to the Divinity was intended, the priest alone had a right to offer it; while, in the form before us, every Hebrew has right to slaughter before the Tabernacle, provided he sanctifies the act by presenting the blood of the victim to the priest, to be sprinkled on the alter in sign of expiation.

It is, therefore, only animals destined for food, and not for purely religious ceremonies, that are spoken of.

Ante ostium Tabernaculi testimonii immolent eas hostias pacificas. They offer up their peace sacrifices at the entrance of the Tabernacle.

Such is the command to the Hebrews.

Fundetque sacerdos sanguinem super altare Domini. The priest sprinkles the blood on the altar of the Lord.

Such is the role of the Levite.

I repeat, if a symbolic sacrifice to the Divinity was meant the priest alone had a right to offer up the victim, and that not at the door of the Tabernacle, but in the interior temple, where none but himself might enter.

Moreover, the explanation which we resist, can only be rendered possible by singular distortions of the text.

Here we have the interpretation of this passage by the Father de carrière, in the approved edition of the Bible before us.

Levitical text:

Homo qui libet de domo Israel, si occiderit bovem, aut ovem, aut capram, in castris vel extra castra.

Et non obtulerit ad ostium Tabernaculi oblationem Domino, sanguinis reus erit, quasi si sanguinem fuderit sic peribit de medio populi sui. Ideo sacerdoti affer redebent filii Israel hostias suas quas occident in agro, ut sanctificentur Domino.

Literal translation:

Every man of the house of Israel who shall have killed ox,

or a sheep, or a goat, within the camp, or without.

And who shall not have offered it to the Lord before the gates of the Tabernacle, shall be guilty of blood, and as if he had shed blood, shall perish midst his people.

For this cause should the children of Israel offer to the priest the victims which they have slain in the fields that they may be sanctified by the Lord.

Translation by the Jesuit Father de Carriere

Every man of the house of Israel, or of proselytes living amongst them, who, desiring to offer a sacrifice to the Lord, shall with the design, have killed an ox, or a sheep, or a goat in the camp, or without the camp.

And who shall not have presented it at the entrance of the Tabernacle to be offered to the Lord, shall be guilty of murder and shall perish in the midst of his people, as if he had shed the blood of a man.

For this cause should the children of Israel present to the priests the pledges they would offer to the Lord, that they may offer them before the Tabernacle, instead of   slaughtering them in the fields.

The italic passages exist not in the text; this loyalty of translation needs no comment. Let us, however, remark that it is precisely these unscrupulous interpolations that serve to support the pretension that Leviticus was understood in this chapter, to speak of animals offered purely in sacrifice to Jehovah, and not of those destined for the people.

Moreover, Leviticus, chap.vii., seems itself to exhaust the question, when commanding that the blood and the fat of all slaughtered animals, indiscriminately, be offered to the Lord, on pain of death; and that the breast and the right shoulder of each victim, immolated, be given to the priest.

Incontestably, then the question here is of animals destined for food, and it is equally incontestable that we must revert to the extreme East for that explanation of these customs which to Bible affords us not.

Impurity occasioned by the dead, and preservation from defilement, according to Leviticus, chap. xxi:

The Lord also said unto Moses,– Speak unto the priests, sons of Aaron, that they defile not themselves at funeral ceremonies on the death of one of their brethren.

Unless ceremonies for those who are most nearly allied to them by blood, such as a father, a mother, a son, a daughter, or a brother.

And a virgin sister, who has not yet been married. But the priest shall not defile himself, even at the death of the prince of his people.

On these occasions the priests shall not shave their heads, nor their beards, nor make incisions in their flesh.

They shall preserve themselves pure for God, and shall defile not his name, for they present incense to the Lord, and offer the bread of their God, for this cause should they remain undefiled.

Leviticus, Chap. xxii:

The Lord spake again unto Moses and said:

Speak to Aaron and to his sons that they be careful, when defiled, not to touch the sacred oblations of the children of Israel to soil that which they offer Me and which is consecrated to Me, for I am the Lord.

Say unto them and to their posterity: whatsoever man of your race being impure, shall approach such things as have been offered by the children of Israel to the Lord, and have been consecrated to him, shall perish before the Lord.

The man of the race of Aaron, who shall be leprous, or who shall suffer what should only occur in the use of Marriage, shall not eat of what has been sanctified unto Me, until he shall be healed. Who shall touch a man defiled by the touch of a corpse, or of a man suffering what should only occur in the use of marriage.

Or who shall touch any crawling thing, and generally all that is impure and that may not be touched without defilement, shall be unclean until the evening, and shall not eat of consecrated things before washing his body in water.

Then, after sunset, being purified, he shall eat of consecrated things, as they only food permitted him.

They shall not eat of the beast that hath died, or been killed by another beast, with such food they shall not defile themselves.

Let them keep my precepts, that they fall not into impurity, and that they die not in the sanctuary after having defiled it, for I am the Lord who sanctify them.

Were it not for our habit of, for the most part, reading the Bible without troubling ourselves to understand its sense, we should long since have perceived and become satisfied that it is but a jumble of ancient mysteries, of which the initiated alone held the keys, and of the most vulgar superstitions of Egypt.

The two passages above cited require some development before following them up with their Indian begotten ordinances

Chap. xxi, ordains that priests shall not assist at mortuary ceremonies, which are defiling.

It is only permitted them to preside at funerals of near relation, carefully abstaining always from what may defile them.

There is no exception to this funeral rule, even at the death of prince of the people.

Chap. xxii, forbids priests while impure, to touch things holy, that is while leprous, affected with certain maladies, or soiled by the touch, direct or indirect, of the dead, or by touch of things that crawl upon the earth, and generally of impure things according to the words of Leviticus.

And this is what they would have us accept as a Divine revelation. The priest is defiled who attends his fellow-creature to his last home. The priest is defiled by contact, direct or indirect, with the dead. The priest is impure because an involuntary sufferer from disease. The priest is impure from contact with crawling animals. What a singular collection of ridiculous superstitions, and how we should shrug our shoulders with pity on meeting such thing in the theology of some savage people of Oceanica!

What! could such utterances have fallen from the mouth of God! The Supreme Being but manifested himself to men to constrain them to such singular practices!

I can understand that, to a certain extent, all this may have been good for this people of Israel, brutified by servitude, and who, in their emancipation, but distinguished themselves in brigandage and murder; but to require us at this time of day to bend the knee to such absurdities would be, I hesitate not to proclaim, to despair forever of the sound preceptorship of human reason.

Fortunately there is nothing easier than to show this revelation that it revealed nothing, and to prove that Moses did nothing more than continue the traditions of the East, and to institute the Levites on the model of Hierophants and Brahmins.

It is to be remarked in the Bible of the Hebrew legislator, that is, in five books attributed to him, that very little is said about the impurities of vice, or if you prefer it, of sin. All defilement comes from impure contact.

Touch not the dead, nor a creeping thing, nor a diseased person, you shall perish before the Lord.– *Peribit coram Domino carnem suam aqua,* is a simple code of sanitary regulation adopted by all the peoples of Upper Asia, by all the peoples of the East; and the Jehovah of Moses in no more the revealer than Muhammad, who also placed ablutions (so necessary in those climates) under the rule of religion.

But ancient legislators found it necessary to make cleanliness imperative upon the indolent inhabitants of a burning soil, and Moses, who leaves not even a hint of their motive, without which they are absurd.

The following prohibition may in fact be pronounced worse than absurd:

"Et ad omnem mortuum non ingreditur omnino; super patre quoque suo et matre non contaminabitur. And he shall never come near many dead person, whatever, be it even father or mother, for he shall be defiled."

I am quite aware, it will be said that I do not comprehend the Bible, that in all this there is a figurative meaning that I do not catch, because my eyes have not been opened by the light of faith; that these customs are but typical, and this purity exacted from the ancient Levites is but figurative of the purity essential to the priests of the new church.

I know all the opinions of Father de Carrière and others, and of their disciples, and I also know their system of translating and of torturing texts, now that they may no longer torture heretics.

It would be too absurd to expect us to believe that all the customs, the usages, the habits of life of a people, had been inspired by God as an emblem, a figure, a prediction of religion which it was his intention to establish at some later date.

Oh! no sirs, we cannot accept your ideas. For God is not the unskilful workman, whose first rude work requires retouching, and when creating us, with that mysterious object which we shall only know in another life, he, in shedding upon us a spark of his Divine Majesty, bestowed upon us a belief the most sublime and universal conscience holds fast its recollection.

Away, then, with that Hebrew revelation which reason can

never accept; and believe that the sublime and touching morals of Christ needs no such precursors as the superstitions left as popular pabulum by the initiated of ancient times.

Manu, the Vedas, and Ramatsariar, the commentator, on defilement occasioned by the dead

Manu, lib. v.:

"The defilement occasioned by a corpse has been declared to last ten days for those who preside at the funeral ceremonies, until the bones are collected. (We know that Hindu practise cremation.)

"The defilement occasioned by death extends to all relations. In one day and one night added to three times three nights, the near relations of the defunct, who have touched the corpse are purified, and three days are necessary for distant relations.

"The disciple who accomplishes the funeral ceremonies of his spiritual directors is only cleansed after ten nights, he is placed in the same rank as relations who have borne the corpse.

"For male children (of the priestly caste) who die before tonsure, the purification is one night; but if they have received the tonsure, a purification of three nights is required."

"A child dead before the age of two years without tonsure, should be transported by his parents to consecrated ground, without cremation, and the parents undergo a purification of three days."

"A *dvija*, if the companion of his noviciate die, is unclean for one day."

"The maternal relations of betrothed girls not yet married, who die, are purified in three days. The paternal relations are purified in the same manner; let them bathe during three days."

"If a Brahmin, learned in the Holy Scriptures, die, all who approached him are defiled for three nights only."

"If a King die, all who approach him are defiled while the day-light lasts, if he die during the day; and while the star-light if dead during the night."

Such in substance are the funeral rules of impurity for those who touch the dead. Let us now see in what consists the impurity of the priest, and in what manner he should purify himself from contact with the dead.

Extract from the Veda (precepts):

"The Brahmin, who has received the sacred investiture, and who is thereby destined to perform *Yajña* and expound the Holy Scriptures, should abstain from all contact with the dead, for the dead defile, and the officiating priest should be always pure."

"The sight even of an impure person defiles him, and he should after the prescribed ablution, recite in a low voice, the prayers that efface defilement."

"But the Brahmin who performs the funeral ceremonies at the death of his father and of his mother is not defiled, for the Lord of all things has said, 'Who honours his father and his mother in this life, and do *yajña* at their death which is their birth in God, can never be impure.'

"If he officiates at the funeral of his brothers and his sisters who have not yet found husbands, he shall be impure until the end of the ceremony, and shall purify himself by prayer and ablutions until the second setting of the sun."

"While unclean let him never enter the temple to offer do the *yajña Sarvamedha* or *Aśvanmedha*, the *Yajña* he will perform will be impure."

"Let him assist at royal funerals, let him sanctify them by his prayers, but let him not touch the corpse."

Abandoning, then, these regulations of personal defilement, which to it appear but secondary, the Veda continues from a lofty standard never attained by the Bible:

"The truly wise, twice regenerated, who live in constant contemplation of God, can be defiled by nothing in this world."

"Virtue is always pure, and he is virtue."

"Charity is always pure, and he is charity."

"Prayer is always pure, and he is prayer."

"Good is always pure, and he is good."

"The Divine essence is always pure, and he is portion the Divine essence."

"The sun's ray is always pure, and his soul is like a ray of the sun that vivifies all around it."

"Even his death defiles not, for death is for the sage, twice regenerated, second birth in the bosom of Brahmā."

Ramatsariar (commentary of the Veda):

"The person becomes defiled from impure contact with the dead, and with all things which the law hath declared impure."

"The soul is defiled by vice."

"These laws of personal impurity were established by him who exists by the sole power of his own will, that man may preserve his physical life, and give it health and strength by ablutions with water, which is the sovereign purifier."

"The impurities of the soul are purified by the study of the Holy Scriptures, by expiatory *yajñas* and prayer, etc."

"And as saith the Divine Manu, a Brahmin is purified by separation from all mundane affections."

Defects which exclude priests from officiating at *yajña*.–(Ramatsariar Commentaries):

"The Brahmin affected with defiling diseases, such as leprosy, elephantiasis, or the itch, may not enter the temple to perform *yajña*, for he is impure, and God will not receive his offering."

"He shall continue impure while so affected, and for ten days after, and he shall purify himself by ablutions in the sacred tank of the temple, and by three aspersions of the water of purification.

"If his malady be incurable, he shall be forever excluded from *yajñas* but shall have his share of the offerings of rice, honey, ghee, for Manu had said, the who shall live upon unconsecrated food shall be cursed in all his successive births."

Thus we see that the sacred books and the theologians of India suspended from doing *yajña* and from the temple only those invalid Brahmins who were affected, with contagious diseases, and that only until restored and purified.

Having copied the principle, the Bible exaggerates its application, and, as usual, with a narrowness of thought approaching the ridiculous.

What can we think of this Jehovah of Moses, who expels from his temple all who have a squint! or who have the misfortune to be born with a nose too large, or too small, or a crooked nose!

In the light of faith, no doubt, will be found the secret of those sadly curious things which so profoundly testify to the narrowness of thought and grovelling spirit of their author.

To found religious disability on a squinting eye, or an ill formed nose!

It was well worth while to abjure the superstitions of Egypt, and to exterminate the followers of Moloch!

But it is high time to desist from these comparisons between Hebrew and Indian usages, not that the ground is wanting, or that texts fail us; but it seems to us superfluous so to encumber this volume, at the expense of other matters of which it must treat.

Besides, the proof of the theory which we mention, that is, that social Judaism was, as in fact were all the other civilisations of antiquity, but an Indian emanation through Egypt, appears to us sufficiently established to justify us in proceeding with the most interesting section of our programme.

After general perusal of the early parts of this work, and in the face of affinities so conclusive, would it not be a simple rejection of demonstration, to deny the influence of primitive Oriental societies upon all antiquity, for the purpose of attributing those resemblances to mere blind chance?

But two ways remain to our adversaries of seeking to reverse these facts and the conclusions that flow from them.

The first is, to maintain that the influence upon ancient peoples attributed by us to India, may just as well have emanated from Moses and Biblical revelation.

The second is, to question the authenticity of the sacred books of the Indian, or at least to assign them an origin posterior to that of Moses.

These two objections which I have already heard produced, are only important in appearance; but it is only fair that they should be examined, and although the early pages of this work were only written to combat them, it remains to demonstrate that they are but the result of a philosophic and historic anachronism.

This question once disposed of, will so much the more brighten those sublime traditions of the Indian Genesis which we approach, and which we are especially anxious not to obscure by discussions that would only tend to diminish their interest.

VI

IMPOSSIBILITY OF BIBLICAL INFLUENCE ON THE ANCIENT WORLD

Some Catholic writer, with intelligible enthusiasm, have bought to make Moses the initiator of ancient societies.

Thinking men, who have dipped into antiquity, will, I think, be of opinion that we might safely deny this proposition the honour of discussion; nevertheless, a semblance of objection might arise from such pretension.

Let us see, then, what it is worth.

I can understand that the influence of a great nation–the Roman empire, to wit – may impress itself upon people subjugated by conquest to its laws.

I can understand that a little people, – the Athenians, for instance, — by extraordinary development of artistic, literary, philosophic, and moral genius, may become the model of succeeding generations, on that grand highway of progress that fertilises an intelligent world, and knows no nationality. Nor will the ages of Pericles and Angustus ever be expunged from the scene of the civilised world.

Can Jadea lay claim to a similar past?

Where are her great conquests, diffusing far the influence of her name?

Where are her monuments, — artistic, philosophic and literary?

Born of slavery, progeny of the parias of Egypt, the Hebrews, long wandering as outcasts in the desert, rejected on all sides by neighbouring peoples who would neither accept their alliance nor permit them a passage though their countries, at last precipitate themselves, burning, pillaging, slaughtering, like a horde of starving savages, upon the small tribes of

Palestine. Who the Amalekites? Who the Canaanites? Who the Midianites? Who the Amorties? etc.,

Such their conquests!

Never did rascal-rout of brigands, of vagabond thieves, so flood their path of ruin with blood. It is true these outrages and robberies were accomplished in the name of Jehovah, which for many is even to-day a sufficient excuse...

In fact, this God of Peace and Love never found his worshippers sufficiently ferocious, his path of blood, sufficiently full. Had some unhappy mothers and their infants been spared, his wrath made the heavens tremble with frightful denunciations against the Hebrews who had not fully executed his orders; and promptly let all the old women and useless infants be slaughtered, let the virgins only be preserved.

Is it sufficiently moral, curiously lascivious enough? I have often asked myself wherefore the partisans of revelation rejected the Koran; but it is true they would there find lessons of humanity which the Hebrew Gordon has been careful to ignore.

Fortunately these scenes of carnages and turpitude did not extend beyond the narrow bounds of Judea; and the ancient masters of Egypt, as well as of Assyria and Babylon, occasionally bestirred themselves to chastise these madmen, who could never live in peace, nor abandon their taste for rapine and pillage.

It is not, then, by such examples, that this petty people, buried midst the nations of antiquity, and at last absorbed in Roman conquest, could acquire influential consideration.

If we review their degree of advancement in literature, philosophy, arts, and science, we are constrained to admit (and we shall bless him who will demonstrate our error) that we can there discover naught but darkness the most obscure, and ignorance the most profound.

No people of earth have done so little, produced so little,

thought so little....

We rave over the gigantic proportions of Egypt's colossal art, even if its productions do not, like those of Athens, command admiration for beauty and sublimity.

We have Indian art, — parent of that of the entire East, — distinguished alike for majesty and grandeur.

Modern explorations have exhumed the hidden sculpture of Babylon and of Nineveh.

What are the artistic remains of Judea?

We know the answer.

The Hebrews had no art. Read the Bible and the descriptions of the temple dedicated to Jehovah. The Hebrews had no poetry, no literature. Read the Bible.

The Hebrews had no sciences — moral or philosophic Read the Bible.

'Tis always the Bible — still the Bible. Everything is in that book.

Well, then, frankly, that cannot content me; and, if I must say so, the most insignificant page of Plato or of Vyāsa, the most simple tragedy of Sophocles of a Euripides, a scene from *Śakuntalā*, a broken arm from a statue by Phydias, or a sculpture of Dahouta, would be much more instructive to me.

Do we not, then, plainly see, that this people of Israel, brutified by servitude, retaining the traditions of its desert wanderings, oppressed by a Levitism as sterile as it was despotic, constantly, moreover, carried nor into capitvity by neighbouring nations, had neither the idea the time to acquire a taste for great things? Hence, when we speak of Hebrew civilisation, we but articulate an empty word.

In what resemblance in Egypt, in Persia, in India, can we detect the influence of Judea? She but resembles those countries in their most vulgar superstitions.

The higher classes in Egypt and throughout the East

devoted themselves to the study of sciences to the pursuit of those eternal truths whose germ was planted in the conscience of mankind. They believed in the unity of all-powerful and protecting God, supreme giver of all good, image of power and of goodness; leaving to ignorance and slavery, the sacrifice of animals, the offerings of bread and corn, which constitute the bulk of Hebrew theology. It is too evident that the Hebrews did but continue their servile traditions, and it would be too absurd to derive from them the initiating animus of ancient times.

Did not the Egyptian and Indian societies exist in their perfection at he moment when these slaves either fled or were driven out of Egypt into the desert?

The India of the Vedas had long since said its last word. Its splendour was already paling into decay.

Egypt was preparing to shake off the sacerdotal yoke, to throw herself into the arms of kings if she had not already done so.

How could Judea have possibly bequeathed the customs, the morals, the creeds, which she adopted precisely at the moment when these customs, morals, and creeds were being transformed and modified by other peoples who had primitively possessed them? How could she have possibly *bequeathed* them to her precursors?

Were not the Hebrews in the ancient world the very last representatives of a purely theocratic *regime?* Were they not the last who retained those castes of priests and Levites, who, on the model of the hierophants of Egypt, governed the people by miseries and superstitions the most gross, and hesitated not to depose kings who would not be the slaves of their will?

The Israelites were the people the most scorned of antiquity. Neighbouring nations had never forgotten their servile origin; and, accordingly, when slaves were required, they knew where to procure them, by an incursion upon the lands of Judea.

It needs but attentive perusal to demonstrate, as we have so often repeated, that the Bible is not an original book. None of the customs which it enjoins are its own. They are all found in the more ancient civilisation of Egypt and the East.

Will it be said that this book introduced animal sacrifice, the bovine holocaust, for instance, into the world? It would be to lie in the face of history, as to forget that these sacrifices were common to Egypt, and Persia long before Moses ordained them.

The system of purification by ablutions is as old amongst Asiatic people, as their world, and their innovation is still impossible.

Further, the Bible is so manifest an abridgement of ancient sacred books which Moses may have seen at the court of Pharaoh, that it constantly copies passages inexplicable in themselves, but found entire in those books of Manu and the Veda, which it has forgotten to examine.

Thus you constantly meet this prohibition.

"The priest shall not touch any dead thing, nor any crawling thing, nor anything that has been declared impure, for he shall be defined."

Where is the special catalogue of impure things, of all that he is forbidden to touch on pain of defilement?

It exists not in the Bible. It speaks here and there of certain impurities of the man, of the woman, and of certain animals, but all that is flooded, right and left, in a confusion of wearisome repetitions, from which it is impossible to extricate the idea that dictated the law.

In the Indian sacred books, on the contrary, we find a complete and special catalogue of all conditions of defilement, and of the objects that occasion it, with the manner of purification, as well as numerous explanations of the idea that suggested such ordinances.

Which. then, must be precursor of the other?

Is it the detailed doctrine, the *raison d'être* of India, on these matters? It is, on the contrary, those fragments of the Bible, hurriedly written, without order and without connection, and which can only be explained by reverting to those more ancient societies, that afford us the key?

That admits no question.

Will it be said that the Bible first presented the grand idea of the unity of God, which none had before been able to disengage from mysteries and superstition?

To that, we answer that Moses did but disfigure the primitive idea which he imbibed from Egyptian theogony, and that his Jehovah, wrathful, sanguinary, and destroyer of nations, far from being an improvement, is but a perversion of primitive belief.

Such, as we shall soon see, was not India's conception of the Sovereign Master of all things.

I have much more respect for the Greek Jupiter than for the God of Moses; for if he gives some examples not of the purest morality, at least he does not flood his altar with streams of human blood.

Will it be said that Moses preserved to us the traditions of man's creation and of the flood?

We shall prove that he did but obscure them with ridiculous fables, which in fact he has never failed to do with everything that he has touched.

What can we think of that Arabian Night's tale which attributes to the theft of an apple the expulsion of our first parents from paradise, and all the ills which have since afflicted humanity?

It must be confessed that human wisdom is easily contented: but with faith in such things it does astonish me that we should presume to pity the ignorant peoples who have retained their belief in sorcerers.

But enough! We have, perhaps, dwelt too much upon a subject which could, of course, only find supporters amongst the people who have inscribed upon their flags, the device we have already encountered on our road—

Crido quia absurdum.

VII
AUTHENTICITY OF THE INDIAN SACRED BOOKS

"Prove to us the authenticity of the Indian sacred books if you wish us to admit your system," will be said on all sides.

With some this demand will be made in good faith, with others as a snare.

I explain.

If a European writer undertook to explain Moses and the Bible, Christ and his mission, with the writings of the Evangelists, to Chinese or Japanese, the logical amongst these people would not fail to reply "All this is very good, but prove to us the authenticity of all these people and their works, for we are constrained to admit that we have never even heard them spoken of. If it concerned Buddha or Confucius, it would be altogether different."

What would our compatriot do? To take but a single example, he would infallibly thus express himself:

"You are not acquainted, learned Japanese and illustrious Chinese, with the book of our gospels. Learn, then, that nothing is more easy then to prove its authenticity.

"It is the work of four different authors."

"The first, Saint John, wrote"

"Stop, if you please, prove to us first the existence of this man, and then you will return to his book."

"Quite right. Saint John was a fisherman chosen by Christ"

"Another name! If you prove John by Christ, first prove Chirst—for we know nothing of him either."

"I bow to your sound reasoning, magnanimous Chinese. Listen, then. In the thirty-first year of the reign of Augustus, a child, whose birth had been predicted by—"

"But it is always the same thing," promptly exclaims the Japanese. "Who, then, is this Augustus of whom you speak?"

"You desire it— be it Augustus. This prince, adopted son and successor of Cæsar—"

"Ah! this is too much," would cry the Chinese, in turn, "you have a perfect mania for names. Could you not prove to us the truth of your book and its historical existence, with-out all these gentlemen of whom we now hear for the first time?"

"Alas, no!" would reply our unfortunate compatriot, "and I see clearly that to arrive at the proof which you demand, I should be obliged to lay before you a complete history of the ancient civilisations of the West. And farther, with your mania for stopping me at each step and at each name, I should inevitably arrive at obscure points which I could not explain, at the names of heroes, legislators, and kings, for whom I could find no precursors."

What, then, would the Chinese and Japanese do?

The party of good faith would say, — "It is true."

Those who had but spread a snare, would turn to their auditors, saying,—

"This man is but mocking us. It is falsehood that is spoken by his mouth."

Let it not, then, be expected that I shall say,—

"It was the Ṛṣi Bhṛgu, whose epoch loses itself in the most remote ages of the East, first collected the scattered laws of Manu, who already had for many ages been held in honour throughout India. After him, Nārada, who lived before the deluge," etc.

Or thus;

"The Vedas, according to Indian tradition, were revealed in the first *Kṛta yuga*, that is, on the first day of creation. The first commentary of these religious books dates back to the holy king Bhāgiratha, contemporary of Bhṛgu," etc.

This would be to fall into the snare which I have just exposed, and would not fail to elicit cries of triumph from certain camps.

"Ha! ha! you mock us with your Bhṛgu, your Nārada, and your holy king, Bhāgiratha. Who may all these men be, whom you invoke as authorities?"

And the trick would be exposed.

And as I could not reply, given in a couple of journalist articles, a course of history of all ancient civilisations (a work which would require a life of several generations), to reduce to nothing the arguments of my adversaries, to book would be thrown aside, without the admission that it is not my fault if so many people live in uninquiring ignorance of ancient societies that have preceded us upon earth by thousands of years;— without admitting that it is not my fault if Greek and Latin are taught without reverting to the mother-language, the Sanskrit;— if ancient history is taught without reverting to the mother-history that of the India.

The general proofs — the proofs most striking of the authenticity of the holy books of the Indians, have been in my researches on Hebrew and Indian societies, and in the comparisons following them.

I have given them, also, according to the Sanskrit, the language in which these books are written, and which had already ceased to be in use, either as a spoken or a written language, many ages before Moses.

Moreover, when we find in *one* country and amongst *one* people, the laws, the customs, the *morale*, the religious ideas, the poetic tradition of entire antiquity — are we not justified in maintaining that antiquity must thence have gleaned its civilisation?

No one people of this latter epoch exhibited a prefect image of India, and consequently no one possessed the entire of those customs which we find scattered here and there, right and left, in Persia, in Egypt, in Judea, in Greece, and at Rome — customs which India alone possessed complete and in their integrity.

And if to all this we further add that primitive language, that marvellous language which has formed not only all the idioms of the east, but also the Greek, the Latin, the Slave, and Germanic languages, we have a right to say: Behold here the proofs of that authenticity which we claim for the sacred books of the Indians! Find, if you can, throughout the world, and no matter on what subject, proofs more impressive or more palpable, especially after having braved the wreck of a thousand revolutions, and survived the ruin of as many succeeding ages.

PART THIRD

INDIAN ORIGIN OF CHRISTIANITY

In this part we shall study the procedure of Christ which we shall explain by that of Krishna (Christna), the greatest of philosophers we venture to say, not only of India but of the entire world.

LOUIS JACOLLIOT

I

INDIAN ORIGIN OF THE CHRISTIAN IDEAS

If I believed in the catholic religion, I should commence by becoming a Jew, and being a Jew, I should lose no time in adopting Brahmanism.

To the Reader.

Religions impose their dogmas, bend conscience under their laws, deny freedom of discussion and of judgement to their clients, and, in the name of God, proscribe all thought which they do not control, all liberty to bow down and to believe.

Equally, in the name of God, reason propounds other principles, liberty of the individual in thought and act, progress of humanity in the ways of the just and the good, by discussion and examination which can alone relieve the future from the superstitions and obstructions of the past.

Physical sciences erred as long as they followed in the wake of an axiom imposed by the religious idea. Moral sciences will have no better destiny until they disengage themselves from revelation.

Let us spurn mystery and revelation as unworthy of his wisdom, of his infinite power, and, strong in the immortal truths which he has infinite power, and, strong in the immortal truths which he has implanted in us, let us not fear to engage in the struggle that must lead to the triumphant, untrammelled reign of reason.

We shall then have separated the Supreme Being and his worship from all the weakness, all the miseries of human imperfection with which man has been pleased to identify him for more than six thousand years.

Such should be the aim of all free intelligence.

II

SIMPLE EXPLANATION

Having exhibited conspicuously the influence of ancient. India, on all the societies of antiquity, proven the moral, philosophic, historic and religious tradition of Persia, of Egypt, of Judea, of Greece, and of Rome, to have been drawn from that great primitive fountain, exposed the work of Moses as derived from the sacred books of Egypt and the extreme East, we shall now see Christ and his apostles recover, whether from Asia or from Egypt, the primitive traditions of the Vedas, the morale and teaching of Krishna and, with the aid of those sublime and pure principle, attempt regeneration of the ancient world which was everywhere crumbling under decrepitude and corruption.

The next few pages are suggested by the impossibility of elevating fable and prodigy to the level of historic truths, and by the desire to restore the true figure of Christ, by disengaging it from the accumulation of superstitions and wonders, with which it pleased the middle ages to surround it.

Far from me the vulgar pleasure of sapping the authority of Jesus as God; a more lofty motive inspires and directs me; and I respect all sincere beliefs which my reason may, nevertheless, refuse to adopt.

And, I have already said it, I will not and I cannot accept other guide than reason, other light than that of conscience.

God has given me a torch, and I follow it.

The past is but ruin, obscurity, intolerance, and despotism.

Let us change our route, and we shall see what the future may become.

III

IMPOSSIBILITY OF THE LIFE OF CHRISTAS DESCRIBED BY THE EVANGELISTS

The life of the great Christian philosopher, as transmitted to us by the Evangelists, his Apostles, is but a tissue of apocryphal invention, destined to strike popular imagination, and solidly to establish the basis of their new religion.

It must be admitted, however, that the field was wonderfully prepared, and that these men had little difficulty in finding adepts to place fortune and life at the service of reform.

Everywhere Paganism was in its last throes: Jupiter in spite of his altars, had no longer believers; Pythagorean, Aristotle, Socrates, and Plato, had long evicted him form their conscience. Cicero wondered that two priests could look at each other without laughing; for two ages past, Pyrrha, Cimon, Sextus, Empiricus, Enesidemus, no longer believed in anything: Lucretius had just written his book on Nature, and all the great spirits of the age of Augustus, too corrupt to return to simple principles and primordial lights, but staunch to reason, had reached the most perfect scepticism, — leading a life of pleasure midst oblivion of God and of the future destinies of Man.

On another side, those old and decaying theologies had left in the spirit of the multitude the idea of a Redeemer, which ancient India had bequeathed to all the nations: and the wearied people waited for something new to replace their extinct beliefs, to nourish their energy, paralysed by doubt, and in need of hope.

It was then that a poor Jew, though born in the lowest class of the people, did not fear, after devoting fifteen years of his life to study and meditation, to attempt regeneration of this epoch of decrepitude and of materialism.

Every one knows the pure and simple *morale* which he preached, and with what avidity the ancient world transformed itself under the new afflatus. To characterise the teaching of Christ is not our object; our business is simply to seek its origin, and to see by what studies the reformer had been able to reform himself.

From the moment we reject the incarnation, to see in him only a man, whatever his grandeur and his genius, we have a right to find for him precursors, as we have found for Buddha, of Zoroaster, for the Egyptian Manes and for Moses.

It is to us incontestable, that Jesus, up to the moment of his appearance on the world's scene, that is, until thirty years of age, was preparing himself by study for his self-destined mission.

Why delay until thirty years of age to begin his work? Why if he was God, remain inactive during the twelve or fifteen years of his life of youth and manhood? Wherefore not preach even from infancy? it would without doubt have been a most palpable mode of proving his divinity.

We are, it is true, told that at twelve years of age he sustained a thesis in the temple that astonished the Jewish doctors; but what thesis? And why did not the Evangelists think proper to inform us? Is not this fact more likely to be, with a crowd of others, the product of their imagination?

Then, lastly, what did he do from twelve to thirty years of age? I ask a question, of which I shall be very glad to receive a solution.

In the silence of the apologists of Jesus, we can only discover an intentional oblivion; for it would have been necessary to tell the truth, and to disperse the mist of obscurity in which they have been pleased to envelop this grand figure. And the truth is, that Christ, during this space of time, studied, in Egypt, perhaps even in India, the sacred books reserved from long ages from the initiated; and with him the most intelligent of the disciples whom he had attached to himself in the course of his peregrinations.

And it is thus that Christ knew the primitive traditions, and studied the ministry and morale of Krishna which inspired his familiar discourse and his instruction.

I think I hear cries of astonishment and surprise even in the camp of free thought.

Let us then reason! it is to you rationalists, and to you alone, that I address myself; for all discussion with the partisans of faith is impossible the moment we cease to acknowledge the same premises.

If you do not believe in the divinity of Christ, why are you surprised that I should seek out his precursors? Born in an unintelligent, because little cultivated class, it was only by study that he could have so raised himself above his compatriots as to play the important part, of which we know in the East, with his disciples. Such is the only logical explanation of the moral revolution they accomplished. But proofs will not fail, wait for them, before pronouncing judgement on this opinion, which is not with me a simple hypothesis, but even historic truth.

Start not form such words; I say historic truth, because if, with me, you reject the revealed, the marvellous, and the prodigious, there remain only natural causes to study; and if in our pervious examinations we have together found a more ancient doctrine, identical in every point with that of Jesus and his apostles, have we not a right to conclude that the latter drew their inspiration from these same primitive springs?

Did not all the great spirits of antiquity seek intellectual cultivation in Egypt? Was not this old soil the resort of all the thinkers, all the philosophers, all the historians, all the grammarians of that epoch? What, then, did they go to seek? What could that immense Alexandrian Library have contained, the destruction of which is not Cæsar's smallest title to the scorn of future races?

Why, afterwards, did the Neo-Platonicians there found their celebrated school, if the ancient traditions of this country did not, like a brilliant beacon, attract all intelligences, all men of thought?

The son of Mary and Joseph followed the current; Egypt was at hand, and he went to learn. Perhaps even, as I am inclined to think, may he have been conveyed there by his parents in infancy, as, moreover, reported by the evangelists, and did not return, whatever may be pretended, until he had conceived the idea of coming to preach his doctrine to the Jews.

Mary, still a virgin, although wife of Joseph conceived by the operation of the Holy Ghost, third person of the Trinity, and Jesus was born on the 25th December, of the year 4004 of the world, according to Biblical chronology.

The birth, foretold by the prophets, was signalised by different prodigies: shepherds, and also three magi from the East guided by miraculous inspiration, came to Bethlehem, to worship the newly-born.

Herod, King of Jerusalem, fearing the advent of the Messiah, who, according to certain predictions, should dethrone him, *sent and slew, in Bethlehem and all the countries round about, all the children of two years and under.*

Warned by an angel, Joseph and Mary fled into Egypt to save the child from massacre, and did not return until after the death of Herod. At the age of twelve years, Jesus astonished the doctors in the temple by the wisdom of his answers.

At thirty, after having had himself baptised in the waters of Jordan, by John the Baptist, he commences his mission and journeys thorough the cities of Judea, preaching with his disciples; during the three years of his peregrinations a multitude of miracles are attributed to him.

He changed the water into wine at the marriage of Cana, resuscitated Lazarus, three days after death; the son of the widow of Naim, healed the lame, restored sight to the blind, hearing to the deaf, and cast out devils from those possessed.

Accused by the Pharisees and priest of the Jews, of exciting the people to make himself king, he was arrested and handed over to Pontius Pilate, the Roman governor of Judea, who sent him to Caiphas, high priest of the Jews, who had him judged and condemned to death by the Sanhedrim, or council of ancients. Attached to a cross between two thieves, he died, pardoning his persecutors.

Three days after death, he rose again, as he had promised his disciples, and, forty days after resurrection, he ascended into heaven, after having commanded his disciples to go and instruct all peoples in the new faith.

Such, according to the evangelists, are the chief events in the life of the Christian reformer.

Common sense obliges me to denounce the bad faith of the apostles in surrounding Christ with an escort of miracles and wonders, opposed to the laws of nature and of reason, with the evident object of captivating the crowd and gaining partisans.

This role had not even the merit of novelty. How many others had, in fact, played it before them, and with equal success!

What! the evangelists are then, to me, only imposters!

That is not my thought. I maintain solely that these man, no doubt with a laudable object, and to assure to success of their mission, had recourse, like all their predecessors, to prodigies and apocryphal miracles to attach to themselves a divine prestige, and that they made a God of the gentle and sublime victim of the priests of Israel.

Ah! were the fact isolated the history of humanity with out believing knees, perhaps we might hesitate about contesting of the past.

It is ever the case, that in reviewing the most remote epochs, we find in all theogonies of the different peoples who occupy the globe this hope of the advent of God upon earth, hope which sprung, no doubt, from the aspirations of primitive peoples, who at sight of their own imperfections and sufferings, would naturally, in an impulse of faith and love, address themselves to the Supreme Being, creator of all things. The primitive legend of Brahmā promising a redeemer to Heva, was but the result of these aspirations, the poetic manifestation of this belief in the possibility of the divine incarnation.

The results of this general belief were numerous. Krishna appears, proclaims himself the promised redeemer, the offspring of God, and the entire of India recognises and worships him as such.

Buddha comes, in his turn, with the same pretensions; driven out of India by the Brāhmaṇas, he goes to preach his doctrine in Tibet, in Taratry, in China, and in Japan, and these countries deify him, receive him as the Messiah expected for ages.

Later, Zoroaster, exciting Persia against Brahmanical authority, presents himself as a messenger of the Lord; and gives to the people his works or books of the law, which he had written under the dictation of God.

Manes in Egypt, Moses in Judea, continue the tradition, calling themselves Divine messenger and properties and the people continue to kneel, and to believe...

Lastly, Christ appears, his life is short, scarcely had he time to preach, when the Jews put him to death; but his disciples survive; following the course traced out by preceding incarnations, they restore his memory by miracle and prodigy, and make a God of his just man, who, beyond doubt, never had such an ambition during his life. But, as we shall see presently they were not clever, and in too closely copying in Hindu incarnation, they persist us to discover the source of their inspiration, and it is from themselves that will come the most conclusive proofs of their preceding studies in Egypt and in the East.

Will it be said, that if the apostles had created their own god, they would not have died for their convictions?

In religion, as in politics, the argument is valueless; nothing is so easy as to make a martyr of a sectary. Persecution always results in placing error on the same footing as truth, and of enlisting for it ardent defenders.

You do not, I fancy, believe that Krishna was a God? Buddha, too, was descended from Viṣṇu? That Zoroaster was sent by Ormuzd? Explain to me, then, how the partisans of these men could have died in defence of their faith, extinguished the burning piles of the East with their blood, and wearied their persecutors?

Tell me the secret of all the victims to all religious intolerance, the secrets of all devotions to the cause of evil, as numerous as to the cause of good.

Tell me how it could be that the first and few faithful adherents of Mohammed fell at Mecca to defend a prophet, who, in the meantime, had coweringly fled before popular fury?

Still nearer ourselves, do you see that energetic figure of John Huss, the Catholic priest, burnt by Catholicism, for refusing to retract his pretended errors?

Why did he not save himself, when he could have done so by a word?

And the Jews of the middle ages dying for the law of Moses, which the same Catholicism recognises, even while proscribing it. And the Vaudois, the Camisards, and the Protestants of St. Bartholomew, and the sinister hecatombs of the inquisition!

Prepare me a list of the martyrs to an idea, while others had on the eve died for a contrary idea, tell me if we do no die with as much courage for error as for truth.

Be assured the chiefs of a revolution never hesitate to die for it, to defy death in the face of the crowd whose opinion they have conquered, and the Apostles were chiefs of a revolution.

Even had they desired it, it was impossible for them to escape the cross, the arena, or the pile, impossible to say to all the Christians who saw them die: "we have deceived you and we are the first to retract our beliefs."

Moreover, in sacrificing life to their cause, had they not a motive, which should satisfy their-devotion? they suffered for the *morale* which they came to found; they died for the regeneration of humanity, and in that were they believers, but only in that.

Since we confront tortures and the pile for all ideas, since all beliefs, all religions have had their martyrs, have I not a right to maintain that the deaths of the Apostles, victims of their religious emprise, prove nothing for the divinity of Jesus?

That divinity was necessary to their work; the entire past was before them to show there could be no success without it, that the people could not be seduced without parade and miracle. After the death of Christ, did they not attribute to themselves the power to work miracles? Who do we expect to believe that Peter continued to resuscitate the dead, to heal the crippled, and to cast out devils?

One example, from many: "Simon, the magician, who himself performed prodigies, having had himself baptised by the deacon Philip, besought Peter to bestow upon him the power of working miracles; having, for that, been cursed by the chief of the Apostles, he separated himself from the communion of the faithful, and commenced preaching on his own account, calling himself, also, the son of God.

"Having challenged St. Peter in presence of the Emperor Nero, thanks to his magic power, he raised himself to a great height in the air, in the presence of a great crowd of people.

"But Saint Peter having addressed a prayer to God, Simon the magician fell in the middle of the public square and broke his legs."

Are such absurdities worth discussing? and will any man of common sense dare to profess belief in such ridiculous fables?

Whence this magic power of Simon's? From the devil, we shall be told.

Poor devil! what a pitiable figure they make of you; for ages you dare to risk yourself on earth, to install yourself in bodies of men, to work miracles, to strive with God... then, all of a sudden, you shamelessly fly before the institution of the police and the gendarmeire... and you are to-day nothing more than a figure of rhetoric for the use of M. Veuillot and Archbishop Dupanloup. [Lord Shaftesbury and Mr. Spurgeon]

There are still some miracle-workers, some sorcerers, hare and there, but they no more venture on great works; the *sixth chamber* knows two well how to exercise them.

Let us leave all these miracles and sorcerers which can only flourish in obscure epochs of humanity, when people, subjugated or enervated by despotism, seek directors else where than in their conscience and in the immortal light which God himself has deposited with us. Civilisation, the progress of liberty, make short work of all those things which cannot support the light of day, of examination and of discussion.

We are about to see how the Apostles of Jesus, rejecting Judaism and inspired by primitive sacred traditions of the East, impressed upon their new Church the simple and pure stamp of antique Hindu society— the social system of Krishna.

All antiquity had drunk from the great fountain of despotic sacerdotal Brahmanism — ignoring lofty Vedism, from which it but borrowed some grand traditions.

The Apostles, on the contrary, and it is in my eyes their greatest merit, had the wisdom to revert to Krishna and the Vedas; and if they had not the courage to reject the marvellous, because the world was not yet prepared by liberty of thought for complete regeneration, they entitle themselves to our pardon, by the daring with which, careless of life and fortune, they boldly preached those pure and sublime doctrine which they recovered from the sacred books of other times.

Such is the truth of these men, whose intrepidity and devotion we cannot too much admire, always regretting that they did not dare to trample under foot the vain superstitions of their predecessors.

This is the channel to be explored. Perhaps I may not make my conclusions as clear as they appear to me. Let others continue the work. Make Sanskrit a classic language, establish a superior school in India, send chosen men who may reveal to the world the thousands of manuscripts this ancient country has bequeathed us, and we shall see if the future dose not confirm my conclusions.

Let us repeat it even to satiety — if those whom we call the ancients were progenitors of modern nations — so was ancient India the initiatrix of all the civilisations of antiquity.

IV

DEVAKĪ VERSUS MARY

The Indian Redeemer, son of Devakī, is named Krishna—
and later, his disciples decreed him the title of Devadeveśa
(Jezeus)!

The son of Mary, the Christian Redeemer, is named Jesus,
or rather Jeousuah— and later, his disciples gave him the title
of Christ.

Devakī and Krishna precede Mary and Christ by at least
three thousand years; the antique civilisation of India resulted
from this incarnation: all sacred books, all works of
philosophy, *morale*, history and poetry, have made it a point of
honour to rest upon it. To suppress Krishna would be to
suppress ancient India.

Mary and Christ have but reached us through the legendary
reports of the Evangelists; and, although the facts associated
with the Christian incarnation were of a nature to excite to the
highest degree the interest and curiosity of the age in which
they might occur, although this epoch is comparatively near
our own, history, and tradition are like wholly silent about
them; nothing, absolutely nothing, announces them to us.
Neither Suctonius, nor Tactitus, nor nay of the Latin or Greek
historians of the times, allude to the extraordinary adventures
attributed to Jesus; and yet it must be confessed that there was
the matter strongly to tempt the pen of these writers.

How to explain this unanimous silence?

It is, as we have said, that all these adventures are
apocryphal, it is that Jesus passed almost isolated through the
world which paid him little attention; and that it was only later
his disciples made him a legendary hero, by appropriating
some Hebrew prophecies inspired by the East, and borrowing

from Krishna his *morale,* and some of the less supernatural and more probable particularities of his life. (The fact, seems to be that there was Chris as such born in the first century. The modern researches have also proved this fact. In fact, Christianity in the west was the revival of Krishna cult during that period. Christ is the synonym of Krishna. only : Editor)

One fact has always astonished me. Through all the sacred books of primitive times of Egypt and the East, the old tradition of the Messiah had passed into the Hebrew law. How is it, then, if the most important facts and miracles of Jesus' life are not the result of posterior invention, that the Jews refused to recognise the Redeemer whom they expected so impatiently —and whom, even to-day, they still expect?

They were blinded by the Devil, some will say. Enough of this old argument, designed to cloak weak pretensions; and, if possible, let us reason, if only for a moment.

Can it be seriously thought that the Jews would not have hailed Jesus, if he had really performed before them all the miracles assigned to him by the Evangelist?

I am persuaded, for my part, that such prodigies would have found few unbelievers, and that Jesus would not have died on the Cross like a vulgar demagogue seeking to excite the people against the established authorities — for such do the priests of Israel consider him.

We are no longer of that epoch when the marvellous seemed an order of nature, and an uncomprehending multitude bent the submissive knee. Well, let a man appear among us, who during three years of his life shall accumulate miracle upon miracle, change water into wine, feed ten, fifteen, twenty thousand persons with five fishes and two or three loaves, resuscitate the dead restore hearing to the deaf right to the blind etc. and see if priests and Pharisees will have power to condemn him as infamous.

But for that the dead must be really dead, it must be no hindrance if he smell a little unpleasantly, like Lazarus; the water changed into wine must be really water; the blind and the deaf, not complaisantly so; that in fact there be nothing reconcilable with physical or natural science.

If the Jews did not recognise Jesus, it was that the sublime preacher was no doubt content to proclaim his *morale,* and give it the support of his pure example, which would be a reproach midst general corruption, and excite against him all those who lived and ruled by the corruption.

Warned by his death, his apostles changed their tactics. Comprehending the influence of the supernatural on the multitude, they re-originated the incarnation of Krishna and, thanks to it, were able to continue the work to which their master had succumbed.

Hence the conception of the Virgin Mary, and the divinity of Christ.

I infer nothing from these names of Jesus, of Jeosuah, and of Jezeus (Devadeveśa), borne alike by the Hindu and the Christian Redeemers.

As we have seen, all these names of Jesus, Jeosuah, Josias Josue, and Jéovah derive from the two Sanskrit words Zeus (Devas) and Jezeus, (Devadeveśa) which signify, one, the Supreme Being and the other, the Divine Essence. These names, moreover, were common not only amongst the Jews, but throughout the East.

It is not, however, the same with the names Christna (Krishna) and Christ, where we find manifest imitation, the Apostles borrowing from the Hindu. The son of Mary at his birth received only the name of Jesus, and not until after his death was he called Christ by believers.

This word is not Hebrew. Whence comes it, then, if the Apostles did not appropriate the name of the son of Devakī?

In Sanskrit, Krishna, or rather Christna, signifies *messenger of God, promised of God, sacred.*

We write Christna, rather than Krishna, because the

aspirate *Kh* of the Sanskrit is philologically better rendered by our *Ch*, which is also an aspirate, than by our simple *K*. In it, therefore, we are guided by a grammatical rule, and not by the wish to produce a resemblance.

But if this Sanskrit epithet of Christna applies perfectly to the Indian, it will not equally apply to the Christian incarnation, unless we admit the name to have been copied with the *morale* and ministry.

Will it be said that the name comes from the Greek Christos? Besides that most Greek words are pure Sanskrit, which explains the resemblance, wherefore this choice of a Greek sur-nom for Jesus who, a Jew by birth, passed his militant life and died midst his compatriots? The only logical conclusion is that this name of Christ was a part of the complete system adopted by the Apostles — to construct a new society on the model of primitive Indian religion.

V

MASSACRE OF THE INNOCENTS IN JUDEA

(A Story Borrowed from India)

Kansa, tyrant of Mathura (>Bathura>Bathula>Bethlehem, Editor) to make sure of Krishna, by whom be feared to be dethroned, commanded the massacre of all the male children born on the same night as the divine child.

Herod, King of Judea — from the same motive, has all the children of two years old and under put to death in Bethlehem and the country round about.

All the records of India, scientific, historic, or religious, the *Purāṇas* the *Śāstras*, the *Mahābhārta* the *Bhagvadgītā* the *Bhāgvata*, testify the authenticity of this fact; whereas the version, equally attributed to Herod, has been handed to us only by the Apostles; that is, by those who had an interest in reviving it.

Contemporary history has nowhere recorded this audacious crime, which all men of sense must pronounce materially impossible at the epoch of its professed perpetration. Never would Herod have dared to take upon himself the odium and the responsibility of such a sacrifice.

Who was this king? Having taken part with Cassius and Antony, the latter had him named Tetrarch of Judea by the Roman Senate. Of a supple spirit, altogether modern, he knew when to change his colours, and Augustus continued to him his throne. But he was, in fact but a simple Roman Governor and the gospel itself does not consider him otherwise in the following passage:

"At that time came an edict from Cesar-Augustus for the numbering of all the inhabitants of the empire. This first census was made by Cyrinus, Governor of Syria, and all went to be inscribed, each in his own village. Joseph went up to Nazareth, which is in Galilee, and came into the City of David, called Bethlehem, because he was of that tribe, to be inscribed, with Mary, his wife, who was with child...."

How admit that Herod, an Imperial Governor, under the Pro-consul Cyrinus, could possibly have committed an act of cruelty so stupid and so useless?

What! in the Augustan age, that epoch of intelligence and enlightenment, a fool, for it is impossible to call him anything else, dares to massacre hundreds, perhaps thousands of children (14000, according to some authorities), all the children of two years old and under, says the gospel! and not a father goes to throw himself at the feet of Cyrinus, or of the emperor, to demand justice, not an intelligent or angry voice raised to protest and to denounce in the name of humanity! Those mothers did not then weep at the spilling of their purest blood?

Rectitude and affection were then everywhere dormant at this moment?

Tacitus, who has stamped for ever the crimes of despots with the brand of reprobation, did not then think such infamies worthy of his condemnation?

Nothing— always a complicity of silence...

Apostles of Jesus, you have counted too much upon human credulity, trusted too much that the future might not unveil your manœuvres and your fabricated recitals; — the sanctity of your object made you too oblivious of means, and you have taken the good faith of peoples by surprise in re-producing the fables of another age, which you believed buried for ever.

Will it be objected that Josephus speaks of this massacre of the innocents? The argument is worth nothing; apart from this writer's well merited reputation for bad faith, he affirms nothing, and does but repeat, sixty years after date, a fact, or rather an error, already accredited by the Apostles.

There is one insuperable truth, that it is impossible to discover, anterior to the publication of the Gospels, the faintest trace of this absurd event, which, had it existed, could not have failed to excite a cry of universal reprobation. No, this horrible crime was never committed!

All Catholic historians, with touching unanimity, have devoted Herod to the execration of future races; it is time to wash him of the greater part of the odious reproaches of which he has been the object, and it will be a meritorious work, rejecting interested authorities, to restore, his prestige.

There is a fact of his life which may be cited as an example for all princes, and which displays a rare goodness of heart, especially at that epoch of egotism and of decadence.

A great famine had fallen upon Judea, Herod sold his lands, his costly household stuffs, and his plate, to relieve the sufferings of his people.

Was that the act, think you, of an infant-butcher?

Catholic history does not look too closely when anxious to stigmatise, but it is only just to recognise the facility with which it is equally ready to absolve all the crimes of its adepts. With what praises, with that base adulations, has it not loaded. Constantine, who, while staining himself with the blood of his wife and her son, protected Christians and persecuted heretics!

To such lengths were the Apostles led by servile adoption of the ancient traditions of the East! they required a second edition of the tyrant Kanśa, and their holy wrath fell upon Herod.

All these turpitudes bore their fruit, and we know how skilful their successors were, and still are when it becomes needful to falsify history.

VI

CHRISTIAN CONCEPT OF TRANSFIGURATION BORROWED FROM INDIA

Christna, to reassure his disciples, who trembled before the great armies sent against them by the tyrant of Mathura, appeared to them in all his divine majesty.

This transfiguration is logical, comprehensible; it was, in the face of a great danger, the best means of restoring the drooping courage of Arjuna and the other followers of the Indian redeemer.

According to the Evangelists, Jesus, having taken with him Peter, James and John, led them up a high mountain, and was transfigured before them: "his face shone like the sun, and his vestments became white as snow."

No motive is given for this supernatural action, only in descending the mountain, Jesus says to those who were with him:

"Tell no man of this vision, until that the Son of Man is risen again from among the dead."

Don't speak of it before the resurrection! Let him resuscitate Lazarus, let him heal the son of the centurion; at the smallest miracle, Jesus repeats this caution.

But pray be logical. If you are the redeemer, why hide you acts, the manifestation which might open the eyes of the people? Why leave to your disciples the task of revealing all these things after your death?

"The answer is easy, and the object palpable, but the trick is coarse.

Consider this petty cunning: the Apostles feeling the value of the arguments, and taking care to have it refuted by Jesus himself.

Explain to us, then, might be demanded by believers, how we never heard mention of all these miracles performed by Christ?

It is very simple, they might then reply, Jesus forbid us to talk of them, and it is only after his death that we are commissioned to divulge these wonders.

Well acted for the weak, the credulous, and the imbecile. But for the others?

It still remains, however, to explain how the thousands of persons, fed with a few fishes, never spoke: how the wedding guests of Cana remained silent; how... but we fall into repetition, it is always the same thing. How stale is all this!

Moses, when he ascended the mountains to converse with Jehovah, forbade anyone in Israel to follow him, on pain of death.

Zoroaster wrote his Nosks, alone with Ormuzd!

Buddha, when he wished to converse with Brahmā, sent away his followers!

Christna and Christ transfigured themselves only before their Apostles, when in public it would have sufficed to preclude incredulity.

And, on the model of all these people who feared the light, Mohammed, the last comer, withdraws into a cavern when he wishes to receive the order of the Lord.

It is to be hoped, however, that all this is over and that we are relieved, once for all, of all these miracle-workers, who hide themselves behind screens to fabricate their prodigies.

During five or six thousand years has the priest ruled the world by confiscating the idea of God to his own profit, and proscribing liberty. It is time to toll the funeral knell of this demoralising power, it is time to abjure the past and to found a truly humanitarian future.

The old Hindu incarnation gave it a shake, and imitators and plagiarists have not been wanting. Let us tear out those last roots which threaten again to sprout from earth for the obstruction of free and rational progress.

Liberty will not imitate the priest, she will not proscribe him but will exclude him from government and politics, and replace him in the temple, whence he has never emerged but as the unavowed instrument of degradation and corruption.

VII

STORY OF MAGDALEN BORROWED FROM INDIAN STORY OF NICHDALI AND SARASVATI

The legend of the holy women, Nichdali and Sarasvati, has beyond doubt, been revived by the Evangelists in the legend of the Magdalen; as is easily recognised.

The Indian women approach Christna (Krishna) to adore him, and the people murmur at their audacity.

The Jewess approaches Christ for the same purpose, and the Apostles would repulse her.

Nichdali and Sarasvati lavish perfumes on the head of Christna (Krishna)

The same act is ascribed to the Magdalen.

The only difference between these figments is, that the first, although of the lowest class of the people, are virtuous and honest, and come to solicit a cessation of their sterility: while the other is a prostitute imploring pardon for her sins.

There again is Indian influence incontestable, although it seems to declare itself less by some insignificant details.

The moral principle is the same, let the weak and the oppressed come to me, justice is for the helpless as for the powerful, for the guilty as for the just.

Sublime maxims by which the Indians, heirs of Christna (Krishna) should have been content to govern the people; and which the priests, successors of Christ, should never have forgotten.

But no more reflections. We may not fatigue the reader with repetition of the same arguments.

VIII

TENTH HINDU AVATĀRA, OR DESCENT OF CHRISTNA (KRISHNA) UPON EARTH TO ENCOUNTER THE PRINCE OF THE RĀKṢASAS — AN APOCALYPSE OF ST. JOHN

A simple question:

All Indian prophecies announce this tenth Avatāra, that is, the coming of Christna upon earth. Before return of the *Mahāpralaya*, or destruction of all that exists, the God will appear in all his glory, for a terrible combat with the prince of demons, or *Rākṣasas*, disguised as a horse, for the purpose of chasing him back to hell; whence he shall issue to attempt reconquest of his power.

"The world," says Ramatsariar, "commenced by a contest between the spirit of good and the spirit of evil— and so must end. After the destruction of matter, evil can no longer subsist, it must return to naught." — *Tamas.*

I make no pretension to explain this belief ; but ask an answer.

It was on return from his travels in Asia, from that country governed by the Brahmins of Zoroaster, that Saint John wrote his Apocalypse. Is it not evident that it was there he gleaned this prediction, unknown to the Apostles, which applies not to Christ, and which makes him return, at the end of the world, like the Indian incarnations, to encounter the prince of demons in the shape of a horse?

The Apocalypse, as may be easily seen, is in its figurative style, its introduction of animals, of elements, and, above all, in its obscurity, wholly in the characteristic cloudy spirit of the East.

Another almost undeniable plagiarism: to point out all would be endless.

IX

CHRIST TEMPTED BY THE DEVIL

"In that time," says the Gospel, "Jesus was led by the spirit into the desert to be tempted of the Devil; and after having fasted forty days and forty nights, he was hungry.

"And the tempter, approaching, said to him:

"If thou are the Son of God, command that these stones be made bread.

"Jesus answered:

"It is written: Man shall not live by bread alone, but by every word that cometh out of the mouth of God.

"Then the Devil took him and brought him into the holy city, and having placed him on the top of the temple, said: 'If thou art the Son of God, cast thyself down, for it is written, he has confided thee to his angels, and they shall bear you in their arms, lest your foot strike against a stone.'

"Jesus replied:

"It is also written, thou shalt not tempt the Lord thy God. The devil took him again and conveyed him to an exceeding high mountain, and showed him all the kingdoms of the world and their glory, and said:

"I will give you these things if you will fall down and worship me.

"But Jesus said to him:

"Withdraw thee, Satan, for it is written, thou shalt worship the Lord thy God, and him only shalt thou serve.

"Then the Devil left him, and immediately Angels came and ministered unto him."

Wishing to speak of this temptation of Jesus I simply cite this fine passage, after the Gospel, from fear of spoiling it by abridgement.

I have not found in sacred books of the Indians the facsimile of this event; but will not affirm that it may not be found. It will be easily understood, that the powers of one man must be insufficient, conveniently to explore all the subjects touched on by this work.

I shall certainly recur, after still more important studies, to many things that remain obscure or imperfectly elucidated.

However this be, and admitting this passage to be the peculiar property of the Evangelists, it affords us the opportunity of too easily catching them in the flagrant act of imposture to be permitted to escape.

What think you of this devil who occupies himself in carrying off God.

Is it God who allows himself to be seized by the Devil?

To what depth, then, may fanaticism abase conscience and the most ordinary teaching of reason, when such monstrous absurdities, such burlesques of the wisdom and the omnipotence of the Supreme Being, are daringly offered to the credulity of the people!

Not content with having himself carried from the desert to the top of a temple, from that temple to a mountain, God, that is the Master of the Universe, the Creator and Supreme Ruler of all things, further consents to cavil with the Devil! and the latter to play the facetious!

Eat these stones, by commanding them to change themselves into bread.

If you are God, throw yourself down from this temple!

Worship me, and I will give you the empire of the world!

And, curiously enough, the pretended God takes the trouble to reply seriously!

By what name denounce such blasphemies, if all these adventures were not simply ridiculous?

The adepts of these superstitions are, in truth, welcome to pelt with the mud of Sacristie and Jesuit holy-office, the partisans of reason and of freedom of thought; it needs their audacity, their spirit of party, to dare denounce us as materialists and atheists, for desiring to divest the grand figure of God of all those unworthy weaknesses invented by the sectaries of a decaying past.

Does not Cicero's sarcasm find application here? can it be that Mark or John, Luke or Matthew, could look at each other without laughing?

Long ago, had these man only adopted the superstitions of India, had they not encountered that sublime *morale* of Christna which illumined the first ages, would they have been consigned to contempt and oblivion, with the priests of Vesta, of Osiris, and of Isis.

The *morale,* that is what saved them, what made their success in the first ages, until the moment when their well secured power enabled them to dictate their orders to peoples and to kings, and to re-establish their regime of denomination.

X

INDIAN ORIGIN OF THE CONSTITUTION OF THE CHURCH

We have said that Jesus and his Apostles had studied in Egypt and the East, that the revolution effected by them was due to the sacred books of India; new proofs, still more irrefutable, will add themselves to those already given in support of this proposition.

We have just seen the material impossibility of all the miracles, of all the superstitions, with which it pleased the Evangelists to surround the life of the Christian reformer, in discovering that they were all but a second edition of the same fact and acts already attributed to Christna (Krishna) by ancient India. We are about to show, in a few words, that the Christian church continuing the same borrowing system, is but a second edition of the primitive Indian church.

Moses, the Prophets, in a word, the Hebrew religion, knew nothing of the trinity of God, in the sense of Father, Son, and Holy Ghost, as introduced in the Christian idea.

Whence did the Apostles imbibe this doctrine of Trinity in Unity? Nowhere does Jesus define it as a serious dogma, he seems to have been much more a partisan of the simple Unity of the Supreme being than his successors.

It is logical to conclude that the Apostles adopted this dogma, with their many other borrowings from the theology of the East.

Brahmā is God the Father, Viṣṇu is the Son incarnate in Christna (Krishna), Śiva is the Spirit who presides at the manifestation of Omnipotence, the operating afflatus.

Here is the Indian belief transplanted into Catholicism, the imitation is flagrant, for it would be absurd to suppose that the Apostles invented this theory of the three persons of the Divinity, when Vedic ideology, which prevailed not only in India, but throughout Asia, had already expressed the same ideas for thousands of years.

We have too long forgotten that Christianity was born in the East, and was there developed before gaining over the nations of the West, and that there must we return if we would discover the sources from which it sprung.

Reference to the chapters devoted to the Indian religion will sufficiently show that the *yajñas* and other *sanskāras* (sacraments) of that creed were adopted almost literally by the new Church.

Is Christian baptism anything else then Bharatiya baptism?

How easy is it to indicate its origin!

The partisans of Christna (Krishna) have a sacred river,

The Yamuna whose waters should wash out original sin. John the Baptist and his followers, have also a sacred river, the Jordan whose waters are used for the same purpose.

This custom, indigenous in the extreme East, the country of religious ablutions, was doubtless so well known to all the world, that the Apostles subjected Jesus to it, not daring to attribute to him the merit of instituting the first of their sacraments.

There was but one means of extrication from the difficulty which was to establish John as the precursor of Christ, by order of God which they did.

But wherefore this precursor? Bah! enough of caviling; what good in dwelling upon insignificant questions.

At sixteen the Hindu is obliged to present himself at the temple, to have his purification, confirmed by the application of holy oil.

And this ceremony is equally made its own by the new

religion — by Catholicism.

As all children cannot be presented at the Yamuna, the Indians substitute for the waters of the holy river, the water of purification, in which they dissolve salt and aromatics to preserve it.

As it is equally impossible, as the Christian communion increases, to transport all the new-born to the banks of Jordan, the Apostles, following the Indian rite, adopt the usage of holy water.

The ancient Brāhmaṇas were religious judges, received public confessions of faults, and adjudged the penalty.

The Apostles arrogate the same functions, and establish the public confessions alone in use, as we know, in the first times of the church.

It was not until more than two centuries after Jesus Christ that the bishops substituted private for public confessions — an occult agency whose demoralising tendency is too easily indicated.

The Indian priest is anointed with consecrated oil, practices the tonsures, and receives investiture of the sacred thread.

The Apostles do the same to distinguish themselves from lay-believers.

Communion did not exit in the Indian religion as a sacrament. As we have seen in our Indian studies, there is a law for the faithful to eat with the priest in the temple, of the flour, the rice, and the fruits which have been offered to God in sacrifice, and this holy food purifies from all stain. But it is not said that God is present.

In adopting this ceremony the Apostles added this last clause, and that is called the Eucharist. It is nevertheless true that this Christian custom was and is but a copy of the Indian usage that the first believers eat bread and drank wine in common which resembled in nothing the actual symbolic Host.

Protestants, who deny the real presence and receive their sacrament in two kinds, parented with good reason to have thus returned to the simple usage of the first ages.

Lastly, to have done with all these borrowings, much more numerous, no doubt, but of which we take only the most prominent.

The Sacrifice of the Mass is nothing else then the Indian Sacrifice of *Sarvamedha*.

In the *Sarvamedha*, Brahmā, victim becomes oblations and manifests himself in the form of this created world.

Does the Christian sacrifice emanate from another idea? Answer who can, or who dare; attacking the errors of others, we shall be glad to recognise our own.

The revolt of the angles, the first creatures created by God, does not exist in Judaism, that is, in the religious constitution of Moses. The revolt of the Devas against Brahmā gave birth to the Christian dogma. India again, always India that initiates!

The reader will understand that we pass rapidly over all these things. Wherefore dally with the brutal forces of facts?

It is as evident that the Apostles copied India, as that our French law has copied the code of Justinian, which itself was derived through Asia and Egypt, from the laws of Manu.

A man during three years preaches charity, good will, and abnegation, confines himself to the *morale;* institutes neither dogmas nor ceremonies, restricting himself to resuscitation of for the men of his epoch, of the grand principles of conscience which they had rather forsworn than forgotten.

The companions, the successors of this man, who was Jesus, construct after his death a complete religious worship; rites, dogmas, ceremonies, new sacraments, are taken neither from Paganism nor from Judaism. Whence come they, then, if not borrowed from ancient India, which possesses the same beliefs the same exterior manifestations, the same worship, and that from thousands of years before the Christian revolution?

This is not all: Jesus becomes Christ, he re-unites in himself all the mysteries, all miracles, all the prodigies of Christna (Krishna). His *morale,* which we only know by his Apostles, is the same as that of the Hindu incarnation, Mary revives the figure of Devakī. Herod copies Kanśa, the tyrant of Mathura. Jordan plays the part of Yamuna. Holy water succeeds the waters of purification; baptism, confirmation, confession, Eucharist, less the real presence, ordination of priests by tonsures and consecrated oil, all resemble, all modelled one from the other. And the Apostles would have us believe that they had received a celestial mission!... And were not inspired from the East, by the antique Indian religion which illumined the ancient world!

But let us come to an understanding. I accept the providential mission of the disciples of Jesus, in the same sense as I accept that of Christna, (Krishna), Manu, Buddha, Zoroaster, Manes, Confucius, and Mohammed.

Only let me be permitted to consign these people to the fables dreams, and superstitions of the past!

And to erect on the threshold of the future as the guide of modern nations.

God and Conscience!

XI

WHENCE THE MONKS AND HERMITS OF PRIMITIVE CHRISTIANITY?

Paganism and Judaism knew nothing of cœnobite life.

Whence, then, the affluence of hermits and anchorites, who suddenly appear in the first ages of the Christian Church?

Jesus did not preach the doctrine of seclusion and contemplation, which enticed early Christians to the desert to live midst privations and penitential inflections of all kinds.

Hair-cloth, sack-cloth, and corporal sufferings from no part of this sublime *morale.*

We cannot place sterile indolence under the patronage of him who sanctified labour.

To the militant, succeeded, as we have seen that ascetic life of the Brahmins, which washed out all stains contracted in the exercise of their ministry.

In like manner were all *Samnyāsis* or holy persons constrained by the law to renunciation of all earthly luxuries, pleasures and affection.

A resurrection of Vedic ideas produced Christian cœnobitims.

We have above given the rules imposed upon earnest Indian who desired exclusively to devote themselves to contemplation of Brahmā. The following passages from Manu apply marvellously to the life of Christian anchorites:-

"Let him (who has renounced the world) renounce the ordinary diet of towns, renounce his wife, his sons, and all that he possesses.

"Let him take with him consecrated fire, and all the vessels necessary for sacrifice, and retire into the forest and subdue his appetites.

"Let him wear the skin of a gazelle, or a coat made of bark, and purify himself night and morning. Let him always wear his hair long, and allow his beard, the hair of his body, and his nails to grow.

"Let him contrive, even from his scanty fare, still to give alms.

"Let him study the Holy Scriptures (the Vedas) unceasingly, endure all with patience, be always resigned, show himself compassionate to all beings, give always, and never receive!

"Let him eat only fruits, herbs, and roots.

"Let him sleep upon the bare earth, on thorns, and on flints.

"Let him preserve absolute silence, even when in the villages begging nourishment for his perishable body.

"Let him not live by the practise of either soothsaying or astrology. (These sciences, we see, are out of date, and were they not bought by the Arabs from the East into Europe?)

"In governing his members, in renouncing every kind of affection, and all hatred, in flying from evil and practising good, he prepares himself for immortality."

And, further adds the Holy Scripture:

"Let him desire not death, let him desire not life, and as a labourer at evening waits peaceably for his hire at the door of his master, so let him wait until his hour is come.

"And when for him shall sound the hour of death, let him request to be stretched upon a mat and covered with ashes; and let his last word be a prayer for all humanity that must continue to suffer, when he shall be re-united to the father of all things."

Such was the rule of Hindu and Christian anchorites, To

cite is to prove — these last were but imitators.

The exaggeration of these Brahmanical principles produced Samnyāsis and fakirs, whose manner of life we have described, as well as their tortures, and frightful self-mutilations.

The same causes produced the same results in Christianity, and we see the fakirs Simon-Stylites, Origen, and others, in rivalry with Indian fakirs.

XII

LAST PROOFS

Even in the time of the Apostles there were man who assigned to Christianity an Oriental origin, and who did their utmost to effect a complete return to Indian religion.

They admitted the unrevealed, quiescent Zeus of the Indians, in whose bosom resided the germ of matter and of all the principles of life.

Then the God became *creator,* that is author of the existing world, and revealed himself in Creation.

The Partisans of this system denied revelation, recognising only an uninterrupted tradition ascending to the cradle of humanity and handed down to all peoples from the extreme East — the birth-place, according to them, of our race. Jesus Christ, therefore, whom they considered sent of God, came upon earth not to reform, but to complete the work of tradition, and recall man to the simple and pure faith of the first ages.

These doctrines were maintained in the times of the Apostles by Philo the Jew, Dositheus, Cerinthus, Simon the Magician, and Menander the Samaritan; and, afterwards, developed in the second and third centuries by Carpocratius, Basilides, Valentinus and Tatian of Alexandira, Saturninus of Antioch, Bardesanes of Edessa, as by Marcion an Cerdon, who professed to have found in Aisa the true sources of the religious idea.

The Apostles, seeing themselves unmasked and threatened in their work, treated Simon, Dositheus, and others as heretics, blasphemers, possessed of the devil, and accumulated upon them all the thunders of the infant church.

When later these opinions sought to establish themselves with new arguments, the Christian religion had forgotten its abnegation and poverty, to ascend thrones, and employed its power through emperors, to torture and proscribe all who attempted to question its origin; thus preluding all the massacres, all the proscription, all the butcheries that ensanguined both Middle Ages and times more modern.

Origen, the most celebrated doctor of the church, believed in the pre-existence of souls in worlds above, whence they descended to animate bodies, and that they came to be purified on this earth from anterior transgression, to return at last to union with God.

He also maintained that the pains of hell were not eternal.

All which is nothing else than pure Indian doctrine.

We see that the ruling idea of this book is not of yesterday's birth, and that contemporaries of the Apostles and first Christians eighteen centuries before us, considered the East as the cradle of all religious ideas.

We have therefore only brought to the discussion new arguments, exhumed from the antique atelier of all traditions.

XIII

A WORK OF JESUITISM IN INDIA

The reverend fathers, Jesuits, Franciscans, stranger-missions, and other corporations, unite with touching harmony in India to accomplish a work of Vandalism, which it is right to denounce as well to the learned world as to Orientalists. Every manuscript, every Sanskrit work that falls into their hands is immediately condemned and consigned to the flames. Needless to say that the choice of these gentlemen always falls from preference upon those of highest antiquity, and whose authenticity may appear incontestable.

What is the object of this act of intolerance and folly? Is it to preserve the few Christian of India from reading these works?

No! I affirm that not one of their adepts, who are always of the very lowest class, is capable of understanding the old sacred language of India, which, to-day, is only studied by learned scholars.

Well, then! the answer which would not be given is very simple, viz., they destroy the book because they fear it, and the they may not hereafter have to encounter it.

Oh! they well know, and especially the Jesuits the value of the works they destroy. Every new arrival receives a formal order, so to dispose of all that may fall into his hands. Happily the Brāhmaṇas do not open to them the secret stores stores of their immense literary wealth, philosophic and religious.

This destructive mania has borne its fruits, and it is exceedingly difficult, without extraordinary intimacy, to induce a Brāhmaṇa to permit examination of the sacred works of his pagoda.

The Indian priest, who knows, his influence over the

masses who is obeyed on a sign by both great and little, cannot imagine but that the Catholic priest has the same power over his compatriots.

What do you want with this book? Is their ordinary reply — it is not written for your nation, and you but ask me for it, probably to take it to the mission.

And hence it is, that the Asiatic Society of Calcutta has not yet been able to collect the entire Vedas, and is not quite sure of the copies it possesses in which many designed interpolations have been discovered.

What wonder? For two centuries has this stupid and barbarous destruction continued, and Indians are warned to be suspicious.

Tell us, good Fathers, what then is your hope from burning thought, now that you can no longer burn our bodies? - to extinguish light?

Be well assured it will shine out in spite of you and your dark and secret operations.

www.ingramcontent.com/pod-product-compliance
Lightning Source LLC
LaVergne TN
LVHW041153080426
835511LV00006B/571